WOMENPOWER
STATUS OF WOMEN IN INDIA

WOMENPOWER
STATUS OF WOMEN IN INDIA

By

Ashok Kumar
Harish

GYAN

ISBN : 978-81-212-0353-1

Published, 2018

Published by

Gyan Publishing House
5, Ansari Road
Daryaganj, New Delhi-110002
Phone: 011-47034999, 9811692060
www.gyanbooks.com
E-mail: books@gyanbooks.com

Printed at: G. Print Process, Delhi.

CONTENTS

LIST OF CONTRIBUTORS

Dr. Ashok Kumar
Faculty Member
NIPCCD Regional Centre
Lucknow

A.K. Jha
Lecturer
SNSRKS College
Darbhanga (Bihar)

Prof. B.L. Sinha
Professor
Bihar University
Patna

C.P. Roy
Lecturer
Bihar University
Patna

Harish
Research Scholar
Jawaharlal Nehru Universtty
New Delhi

H.K. Varshney
Faculty Member
IAMR, I.P. Estate
New Delhi

H.P. Joshi
NIPCCD
New Delhi

INTRODUCTION

WOMEN and their problems have acquired a steadily growing importance in social sciences. Hence, after realising the significant role of women, it is desirable that a greater emphasis should be given for her all round development and as such imparting education and providing employment to this vast segment of population becomes prime need of the hour. But even today, nowhere do women have equal rights and status with men. Although the United Nations recognise equality of women, yet there is a lot of discrimination on the basis of sex. Crushing poverty overlaid with long-standing patterns of discrimination create conditions for women which threaten their well-being, deny their choice about child-bearing, limit opportunities for education and training, restrict economic participation and curtail social, political and economic rights. As daughters, wives and mothers, they are caught in life cycle that begins with unequal treatment, with early marriage and often ends with in child birth.

Bringing women out of the house and enabling them to join the mainstream of national life is certainly an important step. In fact, after independence, it was made obligatory to consider women as a weaker section and the Constitution has guaranteed certain Fundamental Rights and special provisions for protection of women. Government launched several programmes and policies for bringing about all round development of women. However, in the initial stages no serious attempts were made to cover the welfare of women under these schemes. But latter on it was realised that the success of community development programmes greatly depend on the co-operation and tacit acceptance of it by the rural women too. At present, the economic stresses and strains experienced by the modern society have compelled the women to find-out means to augment their family income. The economic status of women plays a key role in determining her social status as their inferior social status is based on the implicit assumption that their labour is generally unproductive and the need for production, particularly in the country-side, calls for new skills. The reality of the present situation however is that the large mass of Indian women face today lack of opportunities to acquire these new skills. It is well established that women are an important component in the complex subject of development who constitute nearly half of the population and can not be ignored for any planned and rapid progress of the nation.

The present edited volume covers diverse aspects of the subject through research papers and articles. This joint venture is a multi-disciplinary investigation into various aspects of pressing socio-economic and political problems facing Indian women. It is an academic exercise undertaken to provide an overall view on issues and problems related to women and includes the valuable contributions from distinguished social scientists to present a more comprehensive view on the subject one wishes to know. Taking women fully into consideration as the primary producers of population, this collection stresses the necessity of according priority to appropriate policy intervention designed for women development.

The book contains 12 Chapters where in the first Dr. Kumar and Harish have reviewed the women's status, their problems and perspectives. It was emphasised that the inferior status of women is established right at the birth. There are substantial disparities in the education of boys and girls at all the stages. In terms of employment women are lagging behind. But even then they play very distinct role in the development of the nation.

In the second Chapter Mr. Joshi highlights a well established fact that 'educating a man is educating an individual whereas educating a female is educating the whole family'. Further, he discusses about the several steps and measures taken by the government for the educational development of women. In the third Chapter, Dr. Kumar and Miss Harish concluded that the vulnerability of women's struggle is reinforced by their lack of education. Only 18 per cent of the women in rural India are literate, and many of them barely so. Without education, skills and access to vital information, they are ill-equipped to assert themselves or demand their due. Their education and training is the key not only to catalysing one half of India's population in development, but also for the survival of their children.

Mr. Jha is of the opinion that the poor performance of the programmes introduced to achieve the integration of women in the development process suggests that policy directives alone do not achieve the desired objectives. Programmes do not get implemented due to the lack of comprehension of the relevance of women's contribution to national development. Further, he argues that the major short-comings noticed in the implementation of the programmes for women with development objectives are : (i) Preparation of the concept that women need only welfare services (ii) That the developmental benefits will automatically accrue to the women as a result of economic development of the family (iii) Inadequate knowledge and skills for designing socio-economic activities for women and in group organisations (iv) Lack of supportive services such as credit, child care, marketing, training and technology for reducing the drudgery.

Dr. Kumar has made an attempt on the pattern of women's occupational participation in twenty selected states of India for both rural and urban areas. He focussed primarily on household and non-household industry occupations and investigated with two-digit occupational classifications. It has also been examined by the author whether women workers are relegated to low status ranking occupations, the existing scope for vertical occupational mobility and identification of the major occupations in which workers are in dominance.

One of the greatest assets of our nation are the human resources. Dr. Kumar and Prof. Sinha has considered women as human resource and have come to the conclusion that for improving the status and to bring women into the mainstream women needs economic independence. Not to be a burden on anyone can give a women immense self-confidence. Secondly, she needs a different kind of education and grooming. Thirdly, she needs to have an access to medical and health facilities. Fourthly, social evils like child marriage, child labour, *purdah system, sati-pratha* and dowry which stand in the way of women's development should be removed. Lastly, the attitude of women themselves has to be shaped to creative and positive thinking. Once women are able to rise above the stereo-typed roles assigned to them, they can contribute in achieving the goals of development.

Another Chapter by Dr. Kumar which is mainly observation based, emphasised the role of a national programme called ICDS in women's development. He argues that effective delivery of services under the ICDS scheme depends to a large extent on the organisational system designed for providing the services and on the utilisation or management of inputs available for them. Again, the functioning of an organisation is not merely dependent on the internal structural arrangements but also on the external factors and environment—social, political and economic. Ideally the organisational system might have been designed to deliver the services, its effectiveness will equally depend upon the attitudes of the people in general, the target groups in particular and the commitment of local leadership to the objectives of the project. However, the scheme, 'Integrated Child Development Services (ICDS) is India's gift to her own future, her own children and their mothers'.

A great difficulty with the Indian political scene is that it is impossible to generalise about the inter-relationship between any single factor and political behaviour. Dr. Kumar in the Chapter 'Women in Politics' concluded that patterns of political behaviour from different regions show different relationships, influenced as they are by inter-related factors like the social status of women, their economic position, the cultural norms and above all, the region's outlook towards women's participation in the wider society. Then again, there are some situations which are conspicuous by obvious contradictions. Today, very few women hold crucial positions. In fact, one of the main reasons for the growth of autonomous women's groups is the disillusionment that arises, owing to a consideration of women by some political parties as peripheral elements, inspite of their involvement in day-to-day political work.

As far as women's participation at the grassroot level institutions is concerned, Dr. Kumar has come to the conclusion that it is not upto the mark. He observed that mere reservation will not solve the problem unless women members are given commensurate power to function effectively. In this regard he has suggested some corrective measures, like (i) all women members of panchayat and other executive bodies must be trained and empowered to exercise their authority; (ii) particular attention must be given to the development of inter-personal communication skills amongst the trainees/community leaders; (iii) efforts are required to elicit participation of women through establishing links between the elected representatives and the development functionaries; (iv) programmes meant for women's development should be linked with panchayat/local functionaries for more effective participation of women; (v) supplement formal representation in institutional structures with other measures such as mobilisation of women and involvement of panchayats on specific socio-economic issues, and (vi) there is need to organise women workers either in a co-operative or any other form whereby production and marketing are integrated, etc.

Mr. Varshney in his Chapter has concluded that there is need to pay attention to the problem of education and employment for women both in rural and urban areas. Literacy and education levels among young women are far from satisfactory. The fulfilment of the Constitutional directives to provide free and compulsory education upto the age of 14 years continues to remain a distant dream as far as women are concerned. In our country manpower imbalances in certain categories (specially among young women) do persist although these are not desirable from the point of view of either the individual or the society or the nation. In order to remove these imbalances, adjustment of manpower resources available in the country at different levels is very necessary.

According to Dr. Kumar and Roy the voluntary organisations have got very wide scope of functions in uplifting women's status. But unfortunately they have not realised the potentialities that they have as pressure groups. The public also has become so dependent on the government for the solution of even those problems which can be tackled by the people themselves. It is suggested that the voluntary organisation have to make sincere efforts to re-establish themselves as powerful agencies to fight the deep-rooted social evils for which they need committed and dedicated workers. Unless the voluntary organisations take an active part in the movement of liberation of women, merely governmental agencies cannot achieve the desired results.

Lastly, by making projections of educated women and women labour force, Dr. Kumar indicates the extent of supply and demand of manpower upto the year A.D. 2001. It presents a grave enough picture to merit the consideration not of demographers alone but of persons in charge of national policy. It is our expectation that the article will draw attention for educational policy and planning, and will challenge voluntary organisations to see their role in this field and intensify their efforts through study, research and experimentation.

Finally, we will be failing in our duty if we do not express our gratitude to the distinguished contributors who have responded to our invitation warmly and spontaneously. A number of colleagues and friends have provided valuable advice and assisted in putting this volume together. We must, however, make it clear that the views expressed here are exclusively those of the authors and not of the institutions to which they belong.

It is hoped that the present effort would be found useful.

for all those who involved in planning, academics, administration, voluntary workers and research organisations.

We are particularly grateful to Prof. Moonis Raza, Prof. B.L. Sinha and Dr. S.P. Jain who encouraged our research and writing. The enthusiastic support given by Dr. M.K. Premi and H.P. Joshi was essential in making the initial idea a reality.

We hope this work will bear fruit and before long, the women of India will find their rightful place in the mainstream of national life.

Editors

1. WOMEN IN INDIA : PROBLEMS AND PERSPECTIVES

Ashok Kumar & Harish

WITH the coming of 'Manu Code' in post-Vedic age, the Vedic custom of husband and wife jointly taking part in religious functions slowly came to be rejected. Women's rights depended entirely on her husband and he declared that she was not man's equal in her own right. "A husband must be worshipped by a faithful wife as God". A married woman was not allowed to do anything according to her own pleasure even in her dwelling place. "When young she depends on her father, after marriage on her husband and in old age on her son".[1] Since the famous dictum of Manu, the law giver, which equates drums, rustics, shudras, animals and women and advocates occasional physical punishment for them has set the stage for the status of women in India.[2] Historians have eulogised the position of women during the Vedic age, when they were considered a moral force in the society and held a pivotal position in the family. The fall in the status of women has been attributed to the Muslim invaders. But history bears witness to the fact that even in the 'Vedic' times, Sita the consort of Rama was turned out of the royal palace in Ayodhya in difference to public opinion. Women have, over centuries, been used, abused and exploited and the scenario has not changed much, as we move into the 21st Century.[3]

The inferior status of women is established right at the birth. The birth of a girl-child is unwelcome as she is considered to be an economic burden. Female infanticide was very common in States like Rajasthan.[4] In the present era of increasing inflation and spiralling prices, when the family size has perforce to be restricted, the pressure to have a male child increases and hence the keenness on sex determination, amniocentesis, ultra sound and hence the justification for abortion. The aversion towards a female child is in direct proportion to the dowry the family pays at the time of daughter's marriage. Dowry deaths are a part of India's social reality despite stringent anti-dowry laws.

Education is not considered essential as woman's traditional role is considered to be one of child-bearing and child rearing. Thus women, fail to achieve economic independence, though they bear the heavy burden of looking-after the needs of the family and participate in economic activities, such as agriculture, cottage industry, animal husbandry, industries etc. The average unpaid work done by women outside their homes ranges between 6.1 and 7.5 hours per day. According to an ILO estimate, the unpaid work of women constitute 24 to 29 per cent of the total GNP in all the developing countries. The sex ratio in India is 933 women per 1000 men according to 1981 Census. The average age for marriage of girls is 18.3 years. Amniocentesis tests are being used for sex determination. Age specific death rates are higher for women till the age of 35. In the matter of education, the picture is similarly bleak. A large number (75 per cent) of women are illiterate. Female literacy is 18 per cent in the rural areas and 47.8 per cent in the urban areas. The drop-out rate for girls is estimated at 55.5 per cent at the primary stage and 77.7 per cent at the middle school stage.

Enrolment of girls in higher education has been almost static for the years 1975-85. There are substantial disparities in the enrolment of girls and boys at the University stage and same is the case with technical and professional education.

A total of 89.5 per cent (1981) of the women workers are engaged in the unorganised sector, of them 82.3 per cent are in agriculture and allied occupations. In the organised sector, women constitute 13.3 per cent of the employees. In the public sector they account for 11 per cent of the total employment and in the private sector 17.8 per cent of the total employment. However, it can not be denied that women have to play a distinct role in the development of the nation.

Economic development is the progress towards an increasingly intricate patterns of labour specialization. In communities at the earliest stages of development practically all goods and services are produced and consumed within the family group, but with economic development more people become specialised in particular tasks and the economic autarky of the family group is superseded by the exchange of goods and services. The position of women differs in many basic features in the community groups.[4] If the nation is to develop, it is essential that the basic standard of living of the people is elevated. This cannot be achieved unless women, who constitute half of the population, are mobilised towards contributing to the national development and growth. This has to be a two-way process, women can not contribute meaningfully in the process of development, until their own development is taken care of.

Women have not belied the faith which has been reposed in them. They participated in a big way during the national freedom struggle. There have been agitations against atrocities on women. Women have launched anti-dowry campaigns. The Chipko Movement has become a possibility because of the courage and foresightedness of women in fighting for a better environment.[5] However, there are a host of inhibiting factors namely, social, economic and political which prevent women from being active participants in the development process.

There appears to be nothing final about the roles that women assume in our society. But we have to do a lot for women because they have been suppressed. They have not been allowed to develop, or to contribute in various spheres, in a world where they comprise half of the population. If that half is neglected and is not allowed to play its full part, nation's development can not be achieved. In our country women's roles have undergone change in the direction of narrowing of options and towards an expansion in opportunities.[6] Women do have to put in hard labour. Many roles are expected of them—responsibility for running domestic activities in addition to whatever they do professionally.

Constraints

The cultural norms that specially affect women's health are the attitudes to marriage, the value attached to fertility and sex of the child, the pattern of family organisations and the ideal demanded of women by social conventions.[7] Improvements in female health status are, therefore, critically dependent on a number of non-health development components such as education, opportunities for skills-building, income generation, decision-making and the availability of basic support services to carry-out women's multiple roles.

Women face high risk of malnutrition, retardation in growth and development, disease, disability and even death at three critical stages in their lives, viz., infancy, early childhood, adolescence and reproductive phase. In old age, they face threats of cancer.[8] However, discrimination starts even before birth in the form of sex-determination tests misusing the high technology of amniocentesis, resulting in a new kind of famicide, i.e. abortion of female foetuses. A Survey carried out in Bombay during 1984 revealed that out of 8,000 abortions 7,999 were of female foetuses.[9] Considering this the magnitude of the problem can be imagined. Thus, social attitudes and prejudices inherent in our millieu which are unfavourable towards girls and women, effect their health and nutrition negatively.

There is gradual shrinkage of employment opportunities for women due to modernisation and mechanisation. There has been a masculinisation of jobs. As a result of low participation of women in India's work force, they are accorded a low status as workers. As a result, there is wage differential between men and women for the same work, and there is concentration of women in low paying sectors.

Empowerment

Women empowerment is fast emerging as an important slogan for the 1990s. This slogan is gradually being integrated with that of participation, advanced so vociferously by many in the late 1970s and 1980s. Participation as a key to development was found to be highly misleading because once concepts regarding women's work were redifined, the invisible women of earlier times were suddenly perceived as 'working' women, and thus already participating in their own way in development.[10] The Shramshakti report by the National Commission on Self-Employed Women and Women in the Informal Sector (1988:93) convincingly argues that :

> While the work put in by the women and their earnings meet the survival needs of the family, their contribution in the fields of agriculture, food production, forestry, animal husbandry, industry, processing occupations, etc. contribute to the growth of GNP, thereby making a direct contribution to the national economy. . . . There is no doubt that women's contribution to the family and national economy is much more than their actual earnings.

As stated above, the work participation of women in some important occupations is very low. Merely increasing work participation is not an adequate demand, for neither the labour market nor the structure of occupation is gender neutral . The labour market favours men over women and the division of labour within the occupation is highly sex biased. Although the principle of formal equality is at the base of bourgeois democracy, it was recognised so, in relation to work, 29 years after independence when equal remuneration act was passed in 1976, and this act still awaits uniform and genuine implementation by the government.

Women have always made a very significant contribution to their societies, but a patriarchal conspiracy has prevented women's contribution from receiving its due recognition. The reason is that society's legitimating myths, the creation of written historical records and the production of authoritative self-knowledge have all been enterprises, controlled by males. The implication is that a self-conscious effort must be made to locate women's voices within patriarchal discourse, to 'retrieve' women's history, to bear witness to their contemporary productivity and to ensure that their labour is both recognised and properly rewarded.[11] Women have been and still are excluded from the production of and representation in many social and cultural activities, but even when they are included they do not receive their due recognition.

Women and Development

Future projections say that composition of work-force will undergo a change in 21st Century. Women who constitute about 50 per cent of the total population of the world will exert to have an appropriate share in the work force. The socio-political milieu and socio-political institutions will assert that the women get their rights and legitimate place in the composition of work-force. It is expected that women will have sufficiently larger share in the work-force as compared to the modern times. This new development will entrust additional responsibility to the managers of different organisations and institutions to notify the tasks which could be performed by the women force in the respective organisations keeping in view the plus and minus points of this segment of the work-force.

However, the government being conscious of the present declining trend in women's participation in employment, is determined to expand training facilities for women, promotion of industries involving women's participation, providing easy credit facilities to women entrepreneurs, budgeting of female labour force as a special component of area development plan and most important of all is the promotion of Women's Development Corporation.[12] At the same time, areas and sectors involving low employment to women are being identified and measures are being initiated to create additional employment avenues for them. Steps are being taken to modernise the traditional occupations of women such as spinning, weaving, match-making, coir-making, cashewnuts, fisheries etc.[13] Steps are also being taken to provide required skills in special lines simultaneously.

So far as women labour class is concerned, various schemes are designed to make participation in processing and manufacturing more conducive on the one hand and to provide facilities through the establishments on the other. The programme of Employment and Income Generating Production Units was started in 1982-83 for setting up projects aimed at income generation and employment on a sustained basis to needy women. This programme is implemented with the assistance of Norweigian Agency for International Development (NORAD). Assistance under this programme is given to public sector undertakings and autonomous organisations for the training component of their projects. Beneficiaries include rural poor women, women from weaker sections belonging to Scheduled Castes, Scheduled Tribes, war widows and widows of employees of the implementing organisations.

A new omnibus scheme, Support to Training and Employment Programme for Women (STEP), for rendering support to women's employment in various sectors such as agriculture, dairying, small animal husbandry, fisheries, khadi and village industries, handlooms, handicrafts and sericulture where women are predominantly engaged in work, has been formulated during the current year.[14] In order to implement this programme, certain broad guidelines and parameters have been drawn up by the department under which proposals from various integrated agencies could be considered.

Another new scheme for setting up of Women's Development Corporation in all the States has been formulated during 1986-87. The objective of the scheme is to provide better employment avenues for women so that they can become economically independent and self-reliant. There are a number of other programmes for women being operated by the Central Social Welfare Board.

In Sum

It is high time that an integrated approach was formulated for the overall development of women folk to enable them to participate in the socio-cultural and economic development of our country.[15] Tne problem of women's development should constitute an important segment of planning process. Any further neglect of this important issue would stand in the way of economic development of the country.

However, there is a need for policy and action-oriented research which ought to have a grassroot level component, particularly focussing on women and their economic activities. Secondly, in most cases, policy-makers at the national level make decisions for mobilization of rural women. Experience has shown that mobilizing people at the micro level with a view to involving them in their own development has more meaning for these people. Instead of policy-makers deciding what rural people want, the approach now should be to ask rural people what they think their needs are and to involve them in both programming and implementation of appropriate projects.

Women's work in family enterprises should be recognised according to status of works and in estimating the value of their unpaid labour. Denial of this recognition contributes to their invisibility and results in discrimination in the provision of the development services. Efforts should be made to increase the relevance of education content for rural people. Education should include information on the productive roles of women as well as men, and should not be sex specific. Opportunities for secondary schooling for girls should be extended wherever they are lacking. Vocational training programmes should be provided on the basis of present and future market needs.

All services for women in rural areas should be integrated and offered as a package programme. The Centre of all these services-agriculture, education, health-care, nutrition, family planning and vocational training must be directed towards improving women's earning capacity, increasing their productivity, and making economic activity less burdensome. Non-formal vocational programmes should not be sex-oriented, and should aim at local market, viz. sewing school uniforms, binding books, making school equipment, should be a part of the total education programme to remove the impression in rural areas that this is a poor man's option.

However the multi-dimensional character of women, ranging from tribal areas to rural and urban areas is contributory to building of an economy. Despite the existing problems and evidences of self made lanes of society, women have risen to venture into modern era of equity, emancipation and enlightenment. Today this most efficient work force is facing challenges at construction sites and industrial complexes and in the technological world while working out of the domestic environment.

REFERENCES

1. Sushma Sapru (1989) : 'Socio-Economic Status of Women', in edited book of R.K. Sapru, *Women and Development*, Ashish Publishing House, New Delhi, p. 232.
2. *Ibid.*, p. 233.
3. Vandana Kumari Jena (1989): 'Women and Development', *The Indian Journal of Public Administration*, Oct.-Dec. 1989, Vol. XXXV, No. 4, p. 977.
4. Ashok Kumar (1989) : *Indian Women Towards 21st Century*, Criterion Publications, New Delhi. p. 2.
5. Jena (1989) Op. cit., p. 979.
6. R.K Sapru (1989) Op. cit., p. 275.
7. Govt. of India (1988) : *National Perspective Plan—1988-2000 A.D.*, Min. of HRD, Deptt. of Women and Child Development, New Delhi, p. 97.
8. *Ibid.*, p. 97.
9. *Ibid.*, p. 98.
10. Amar Jesani (1990) : 'Limits of Empowerment—Women in Rural Health Care,' *Economic and Political Weekly*, May 19, 1990, p. 1098.
11. Patricia Uberoi (1990) : 'Feminine Identity and National Ethos in Indian Calendar Art', *Economic and Political Weekly*, April 28, 1990. p. 41.
12. Falendra K. Sudan & Nirmal K. Gupta (1990) : *Women at Work in Developing Economy*, Anmol Publications, New Delhi.
13. *Ibid.*, p. 2.
14. *Ibid.*, p. 147.
15. S.N. Agarwala (1972) : *India's Population*, Bombay Tata McGraw Hill, 1972. p. 4.
16. *Ibid.*, p. 25.

2. EDUCATING WOMEN TO EDUCATE FAMILY

H.P. Joshi

'IF we are educating a man, we are educating an individual whereas if we are educating women, we are educating the whole family'. It is in this view, since independence, the policy-makers have argued for universal education and for making education as a tool for bringing about social equality. Efforts have been made during different plan periods to enrol more girls in schools, to continue their education as long as possible, and to provide non-formal education opportunities for women. Education is the most important instrument for human resource development. Education of women, therefore, occupies top priority amongst various measures taken to improve the status of women in India. In recent years. however, the focus of planning has shifted from equipping women for their traditional roles of house-wives and mother to recognising their worth as producer and making a major contribution to the family.

Education enables women to acquire basic skills and abilities, and fosters a value system which is conducive to raising their status in society. Recognising this fact, great emphasis has been laid on women's education in the Five Year Plans. The First Five Year Plan advocated the need for adopting special measures for solving the problems of women's education. It held that women "must have the same opportunities as men for taking all kinds of work and this presupposes that they get equal facilities so that their entry into the professions and public services is in no way prejudiced". It further added that "at the secondary and even at the university stage it should have a vocational or occupational basis, as far as possible, so that those who complete such stages may be in a position, if necessary, to immediately take up some vocation or other". Accordingly, the educational facilities for girls continued to expand in the subsequent plans. The major schemes undertaken encompassed elementary education, secondary education, university education, post-graduate education and research, technical education, scholarships, social/adult education and physical education. The Second Plan continued the emphasis on overall expansion of educational facilities. The Report of the National Committee On Women's Education (1959) made a strong impact on the Third Five Year Plan. It launched important schemes like condensed school courses for adult women, Bal Sevika training and child-care programmes. Subsequent plans supported these measures and also continued incentives such as free text-books and scholarships for girls. This trend continued in the Fourth and Fifth Five Year Plans.[1]

Although there was a large scale expansion of facilities for education upto the Fourth Plan, vast disparities existed in the relative utilization of available facilities by boys and girls at various stages of education. Hence, the major thrust in the Fifth Plan was to offer equality of opportunities as part of the overall plan of ensuring social justice and improving the quality of education imparted. To promote enrolment and retention in schools in backward areas and among under-privileged sections of the population, in addition to the incentives like free distribution of text-books, mid-day meals etc., girls were to be given uniforms and attendance scholarships. Inspite of these schemes, it was noticed that insufficient number of women teachers resulted in low enrolment of girls. To remove this bottle-neck, scholarships were given to local girls to complete their education and training leading to a teaching career. Besides, condensed and correspondence courses were organized for the less educated women. Emphasis was also laid on the need for orientation of the curriculum to meet the special needs of girls.[2]

A landmark in the Sixth Plan was the inclusion of women's education as one of the major programmes under Women and Development which was an outcome of the publication of the report of the Committee on the Status of Women in India. The programmes for universalization of elementary education were specially directed towards higher enrolment and retention of girls in schools. It was envisaged to promote balwadi-cum-creches attached to the schools to enable girls responsible for sibling care at home to attend schools. Women teachers, where necessary, were to be appointed in rural areas to encourage girls' education. Science teaching in girls schools and colleges had to be strengthened to achieve greater participation of women in science and technology. Streamlining the admission policies to promote greater enrolment of women in engineering, electronics, agriculture, veterinary, fishery and forestry courses was stressed. For boosting the education of women belonging to backward classes, the number of girls' hostels were to be increased. Instead of adding more separate women's polytechnics, which were developed as multi-purpose institutions for imparting training in arts, crafts, etc., co-educational institutions were encouraged as far as possible. The adult education programme too received a fillip.[3]

The Seventh Plan envisages restructuring of the educational programmes and modification of school curricula to eliminate gender bias. Enrolment of girls in elementary, secondary and higher education courses, formal as well as non-formal, has been accorded high priority. At the elementary stage, education has been made free for girls. Sustained efforts are to be made through various schemes and measures to reach 100 per cent coverage in elementary education.

Financial assistance schemes to voluntary agencies to run early childhood education (pre-school centres), the adjuncts of primary/middle schools are to be expanded, particularly to help evolve innovative models suited to specific learner groups or areas. Efforts are to be made to enrol and retain girls in schools, especially in rural areas, and also to enrol children belonging to Scheduled Castes, Scheduled Tribes and other weaker sections. Teacher training programmes are to receive continued priority with a view to increase the availability of trained women teachers, and thereby enhance girl's enrolment and retention in schools. Incentives by way of distribution of uniforms, free text-books and attendance scholarships to needy girls are to be continued. Non-formal elementary education is to be expanded to benefit girls in the age-group of 6-14 years. Talented girls are to be encouraged to pursue higher education. It is also proposed to expand the 'Open Learning System', including correspondence courses for them. In order to promote technical and vocational education for girls, more women's polytechnics are to be set up and programmes for vocationalization of education are to be expanded.[4]

To expedite education among the girls of the Scheduled Castes and Scheduled Tribes, additional facilities will continue to be provided under the "Development of Backward Classes" sector. Girls above the matriculation stage will get higher scholarships/stipends than boy students. Financial assistance is envisaged for construction of hostel buildings for girls at the district level and for purchase of equipment, furniture, utensils, books and periodicals in these hostles.

However, under the National Sports Policy, participation of women and girls in sports and games is to be encouraged. Stress is to be laid on the identification of sports talent among women, and provision made for sports scholarships, coaching and nourishment support for promising girls with a view to improve the standards of their performance in competition, health, nutrition and family planning. An effort was made to build up awareness about these subjects among women through discussions, talks, and distribution of relevant literature.[5]

Under the Adult Education Programme, apart from increasing adult literacy, the content of education was to be modified to incorporate new value systems regarding the role of women in the family and community. The Seventh Plan also envisages, among other schemes, the preparation of district level plans with local community participation both for activating and implementing the literacy programme, and the creation of special mechanisms to monitor the progress of implementation at the State level. The Integrated Rural Development Programme (IRDP), National Rural Employment Programme (NREP), Training of Rural Youth in Self-Employment (TRYSEM), and other such programmes, are also to have a component of functional literacy for women beneficiaries. The programme of Functional Literacy for Adult Women (a component of the ICDS programme) was unfortunately abandoned, though the concept of utilising *Anganwadi* workers, who belonged to the villages and were in contact with young mothers, could have been an effective mechanism for imparting non-formal education. The scheme has since been revised to focus on issues of immediate relevance to women but has yet to be introduced.[6]

However, the various programmes have not yet been able to make any significant impact on literacy levels of the Indian population, particularly on women. According to a World Bank Report, in A.D. 2000 there will be 500 million illiterates in India, constituting 54 per cent of the world's population of illiterates. As per the Seventh Plan, the total number of adult illiterates is about 900 lakhs, of whom 580 lakhs are women.[7] Although it is encouraging to note that the proportion of women in the adult education centres has gone above 50 per cent (52.34 per cent in 1984-85), women still constitute about 57 per cent of the illiterate population. Among these, literacy levels of SC and ST women are still worse. Even those treated as literates, have very low levels of literacy, scant opportunities for continuing education and use of literacy skills. Therefore, they often relapse into illiteracy.

The National Policy on Education, 1986 is a landmark in its approach to women's education. It has attempted for the first time to address itself to the basic issues of women's equality. In the section titled "Education for women's Equality", the policy states :

> Education will be used as an agent of basic change in the status of women. In order to neutralize the accumulated distortions of the past, there will be a well-conceived edge in favour of women. The National Education System will play a positive, interventionist role in the empowerment of women. It will foster the development of new values through redesigned curricula, text-books, training and orientation of teachers, decision-makers and administrators.

It gives over-riding priority to the removal of women's illiteracy and obstacles inhibiting their access to and retention in elementary education. Emphasis has been laid on women's participation in vocational, technical and professional education at different levels as also to promote women's participation in non-traditional occupations and existing and emergent technologies.

So many measures have been suggested to achieve the stated objectives of the National Policy on Education (NPE). The Action Plan enunciates that every educational institution should take up by 1995 active programmes for the development of women. All teachers and non-formal adult education instructors should be trained as agents of women's development. Special programmes should be developed by research institutions to promote general awareness and positive self-image amongst women through programmes like discussions, street plays, wall papers, puppet shows, etc. Preference in recruitment of teachers up to school level should be for women.

National Literacy Mission (NLM) which aims at eradication of illiteracy in 15-35 age-group by 1995 concretises what is envisaged in NPE as regards literacy and adult education.

The Mission document emphasises the importance of imbibing the values of national integration, conservation of environment, women's equality, observance of small family norm etc., and goes on to say that "the focus of NLM would be on rural areas, particularly women and persons belonging to the Scheduled Castes and Scheduled Tribes."

For universalisation of elementary and adult education, the present programme of non-formal centres for girls needs to be extended to all educationally backward pockets of the country. Increased assistance should be given to voluntary organisations to run non-formal education centres for girls. In rural areas, special support services should be provided to relieve the girls from sibling care and other household work like fetching water, fuel. Skill development linked to employment opportunities in the villages is required to be given priority so that there is an incentive on the part of the parents to educate girls. It is necessary to develop adult education programmes for women linked with upgradation of their skills and income generating activities. Skill development for girls should be a continuous process of learning and should be supported by programmes administered by other agencies such as polytechnics Industrial Training Institutes (ITIs), Women's Centres in Agricultural and Home Science Colleges, etc. Continuing Education Centres should be set up in a phased manner to organize vocational training, provide opportunities for retention of literacy skills, and application of this learning for improving their living conditions. There are 104 ITIs functioning exclusively for women and 97 wings in general ITIs reserved for women. These would need to be revamped in terms of diversification of trades and courses, keeping in view the job potential, and facilities for vocational counselling, imparting information about credit, banking, entrepreneurial development and women's access to technical education.

Women's issues would be incorporated in courses under various disciplines. Research should be encouraged on identified areas/subjects. Seminars/workshops should be organized on the need for women's studies, and for dissemination of information and interaction. Educational institutions should be encouraged to take-up programmes like adult education, awareness building, legal literacy, information and training support for socio-economic programmes of women's development, instructional programmes through media, which directly benefit the community and bring about the empowerment of women.

The strategy to be adopted for raising literacy levels and education among women has to keep in view the vast cultural, geographical and ecological variations as also the problems relating to poverty and ignorance. The cultural and geographical variations call for decentralization of educational planning. Within the national perspective, planning, implementation and monitoring of educational programmes has to be done at district and block levels, keeping in view the socio-economic and geographic parameters of the area. The vocational and occupational components have to be designed in accordance with the availability of resources and job opportunities in the regions. Voluntary organizations and women's groups active in the area should be involved in the task.

In view of the social and cultural handicaps that have operated against women's education and taking account of the multiple roles that women are required to play, the need for adopting a set of objectives specific to women's education is imperative. The objectives to be achieved by A.D. 2000 in regard to women's education are :

(i) Elimination of illiteracy, universalisation of elementary education and minimization of dropout rate in the age group of 6-14 years and stagnation to negligible proportions,

(ii) Ensuring opportunities to all women for access to appropriate level, nature and quality of education and also the wherewithal for success comparable with men,

(iii) Substantial vocationalization and diversification of secondary education so as to provide a wide scope for employment and economic independence of women,

(iv) Making education an effective means for women's equality by (a) Addressing ourselves to the constraints that prevent women from participating in the educational process (b) Eliminating the existing sexist bias in the system (c) Making necessary intervention in the content and processes of education to inculcate positive and egalitarian attitudes and (d) Ensuring that teachers' perceive this as one of their essential roles,

(v) Providing non-formal and part-time courses to women to enable them to acquire knowledge and skills for their social, cultural and economic advancement,

(vi) Impetus to enrol in various professional degree courses so as to increase their number in medicine, teaching, engineering and other fields substantially, and

(vii) Creating a new system of accountability, particularly in respect of the basic educational services, to the local community, inter alia, by active involvement of women.

In brief, it is reiterated that the goals and strategies spelt out in the National Policy on Education, POA and the National Literacy Mission will ensure a much larger access for women to education.

High priority has to be accorded to creating awareness, through various communication media, of the need for women's education and their active participation in economic and political development of the nation.

What is needed is not merely larger resource allocation but technical inputs for greater effectiveness of these programmes to guarantee better resource utilization. Emphasis has to be placed on more effective planning, monitoring and evaluation of existing programmes through a result oriented mechanism operating at different levels. Recognizing that a critical input for women's development would be a new thrust to training and wider dissemination of information backed by research data and documentation, it is proposed to set up a National Resource Centre for Women. This resource Centre would translate national developmental needs of women into a systematic grid of programmes and schemes for training at different levels in skills/knowledge/attitudes. The Centre would identify and if necessary, strengthen existing governmental and non-governmental agencies including women's universities, women's centres and colleges through which the training, research/dissemination could be carried out. The National Commission on Self-Employed Women and Women in Informal Sector has also recommended the need for a National Institute to cater to women's training as well as to formulate guidelines and to help the other constituent units at the State level, divisional level and district level to carry out training programmes.

Reorientation and sensitization of administrative machinery at all levels in the Government of India, the States, as well as specialized technical agencies (both government and voluntary) to the issues of women in development is essential. Three levels of orientation is necessary, i.e. at the policy and planning level at the district or intermediary level, and at the block and village level. The training of functionaries and their orientation to women's issues must also be in the right perspective, i.e. women should be perceived as producers and participants, not clients for welfare. The dynamic role of women's contribution to the national economy as partners and equal citizens must be reiterated and translated into programmes and projects. The National Resource Centre would be responsible for revamping the existing content methodology and monitoring of training at all levels. A special division should be created in the Department of Women and Child Development for the enforcement of law for women. The officer in charge may be designated Commissioner for Women's Rights and must liaise with the various Special Cells for women created by the police, the CBI as well as with the Departments of Public Grievances at Centre and State levels as also the Women's Cell in the Home Ministry. This division will be concerned with the enforcement of law to ensure women's rights, to facilitate action oriented research in fields such as discrimination against women, protection at work, etc.

REFERENCES

1. Govt. of India (1988) : National Perspective Plan for Women : 1988-2000 A.D., Ministry of HRD, Deptt. of Women & Child Development, New Delhi.
2. *Ibid.*, p. 70.
3. *Ibid.*, p. 71.
4. *Ibid.*, p. 71.
5. *Ibid.*, p. 75.
6. A. Kumar (1988) : *Indian Women Towards 21st Century*, Criterion Pub., New Delhi.
7. *Ibid.*, p. 11.

3. WHAT THE OTHER HALF DOES ?

Ashok Kumar & Harish

A COMMON myth about women is that they are non-workers. In reality the women of the developing world are not only responsible for producing and in many countries marketing most of its crops, but are also the principal providers of its health-care and a multitude of services related to the family.[1] As UNICEF puts it, "They already bear and care for the third world's children. They make, wash and mend the third world's clothes. They clean the third world's homes, collect the third world's fuel, cook the third world's food, fetch the third world's water and look-after the third world's sick." Equally true as the National Perspective Plan for Women 1988, observes that 'for the majority of women in the country, there is more work than wages, more load than capacity, more compulsion than choice'.

The relevant legislation merely enables States to make it effective but does not require them to enforce it. An estimated 80 per cent of India's women for whom laws have been designed, live and work in the rural areas, where their work-force, participation rate according to the 1981 Census is 16 per cent, while it is only 7.3 per cent for women in urban areas.[2] The National Commission on Self-Employed Women and Women in the Unorganised Sector in its report, Shramshakti, indicates that these figures are highly depressed and estimated that female workers constitute about one-fourth of the total work-force in the economy.

According to the report 79.4 per cent of these workers are engaged in agricultural activities, usually employed at the bottom rung as agricultural labour. The remaining are concentrated in work areas which include livestock production, fisheries, forestry and household industries. An overwhelming proportion of women, 93 per cent or more, can be traced to the unorganised informal sector. Here, bereft of the advantages of the organised sector, including the protection of trade unions, they are left to their resources and are open to exploitation.

The vulnerability of women struggling to survive is reinforced by their lack of education. Nearly 18 per cent of women in rural India are literate, and many of them barely so. Without education, skills and access to vital information, they are ill-equipped to assert themselves or demand their due. Their education and training is the key, not only to catalysing one half of India's population in development, but also to the survival of their children.

Women's Role in Economy

Despite concerted efforts at improving the status of women, Indian women are lagging behind in many spheres.[3] It has been emphatically articulated in many debates among forums connected with the development of women that the Indian society has not succeeded in framing the required norms for institutions to enable women to fulfil the multiple roles (as a mother, housewife and a unit of human capital) that they are expected to play.[4] However, after realising the significant role of women, it is desirable that a greater emphasis should be given for her all round development.

In the male dominating society, the condition of women

depends crucially on the extent of economic independence of females.[5] With this awareness, the present section proposes to analyse available evidence on trends in economic participation with a view to identifying critical issues for further consideration. While the data on female participation rates in urban India is more reliable, one cannot ignore the issue of women's work and employment in rural India. Hence, in the present section we shall confine our discussion to some of the issues related to women's contribution to rural economy.

The long term trend in economic participation of women indicates an overall decline in percentage of workers to total female population in their percentage to the total labour force after 1921, and a slight increase from 1971 to 1981 (Table 3.1).

TABLE 3.1

Percentage of Economically Active Population

Census	Male	Female
1901	61.11	31.70
1911	61.90	33.73
1921	60.52	32.67
1931	58.27	27.63
1941	DNA	DNA
1951	54.05	23.30
1961	57.10	37.96
1971	52.75	14.15
1981	52.65	19.76

The above table reveals that work participation rates have been falling since last half a century, both for males and females. But the fall is sharper for females. Agriculture continued to receive the burden of the surplus labour force all through the period of 81 years. Variation in participation rates in agriculture during different decades mainly show a slight decline before 1947 and a steady rise after that. However, estimates of female participation rates (here in after referred to as FPRs) in rural India are derived from two basic sources, namely the decennial population censuses and the national sample surveys. All of these relate only to those workers whose 'main activity was work'.

It is evident from Table 3.2 that a dramatic decline in the FPR, from 31 per cent to 13 per cent between 1961 and 1971 for India as whole ; a similar decline was witnessed in each of the States too ; this is not a real decline but an apparent one, attributable to changes in the definition of a worker between the 1961 and 1971 censuses.

Now, let us have a look at the 1981 census estimates and see how these compare with the earlier ones. Main workers were defined in the same way as in the 1971 census, namely, if they had worked for a major part of the year preceding the date of enumeration.[7] The FPR, exclusive of marginal workers, increased from 13.4 to 16.5 over the decade (1971 to 1981).[8] These estimates of FPR are for all age-groups taken together. The age-wise break-up of workers and of population for 1981 is not available. In order to analyse changes in the FPR it is necessary to include marginal workers, as the 'main workers' category tends to exclude a lot of female workers who perceive 'non-work' as their main activity. If we include marginal workers, the increase in the FPR between 1971 and 1981 is much greater from 15.9 per cent in 1971 to 23.9 per cent in 1981, than in the FPR of 'main workers' over the same time period.[9] Once again, this does not signify a 'real' increase in FPRs. The dramatic decline in FPR from 1961 to 1971 and the subsequent increase between 1971 and 1981 are not real, as there has been no dramatic change in the extent and or nature of female employment.

Let us turn to the alternative source i.e. NSSO. Between 1972-73 and 1977-78 there was some decline in FPRs for India as whole, though this does not hold for individual States. Between 1977-78 and 1983 there was not much change, with the exception of Jammu & Kashmir. From the above discussion, it is clear that inter-temporal comparability poses a high problem. The number of actual women workers is likely to be quite high in rural India and the available statistics do not capture all of them. This, in turn, is due to the fact that neither society nor the women themselves perceive their role

TABLE 3.2

Female Participation Rates in Rural Areas—Main and Marginal Workers All India & States

India/States	Percentage of Rural Female workers to Total Female population in Rural Areas			Main and Marginal Workers (Female)			
	1961	1971	1981	1971	1977-78	1981	1983
1	2	3	4	5	6	7	8
All-India	31.4	13.4	16.5	15.8	38.5	23.5	38.7
Andhra Pradesh	46.0	27.4	32.9	31.9	54.7	44.9	53.4
Assam	32.4	5.6	N.A.	5.6	13.5	N.A.	13.7
Bihar	28.5	9.3	9.3	10.3	24.5	14.5	27.3
Gujarat	34.1	12.1	14.5	15.2	45.2	26.3	43.3
Jammu & Kashmir	29.5	4.2	N.A.	6.8	44.3	N.A.	29.0
Karnataka	36.8	15.8	22.6	19.0	43.5	30.8	46.3
Kerala	20.9	14.1	13.5	15.3	46.3	18.2	34.3

(*Contd.*)

1	2	3	4	5	6	7	8
Madhya Pradesh	48.6	20.7	26.1	25.1	49.8	35.5	51.6
Maharashtra	46.7	24.4	31.9	28.9	54.6	40.8	51.8
Orissa	27.4	6.8	11.3	15.2	31.4	20.9	23.6
Punjab	16.5	1.4	3.7	2.0	31.6	12.0	31.2
Rajasthan	40.8	9.3	10.7	16.0	65.7	25.0	53.9
Tamil Nadu	37.1	17.6	28.1	20.4	50 9	34.5	51.0
Utter Pradesh	19.9	7.3	6.5	7.7	24.9	10.6	30.0
West Bengal	10.6	4.6	6.3	4.6	20.3	9.4	22.6

India/States	Female Participation Rates Based on NSS Data					
	Usual Status			Current Weekly Status		
	1972-73	1977-78	1983	1972-73	1977-78	1983
1	9	10	11	12	13	14
All-India	37.5	28.8	28.4	30.5	25.9	25.0
Andhra Pradesh	62.5	45.4	46.1	37.0	39.0	37.9
Assam	9.0	7.5	7.9	6.9	6.6	8.2
Bihar	23.0	19.1	17.4	18.5	15.2	15.7
Gujarat	44.5	33.4	34.8	39.8	32.6	32.8
Jammu & Kashmir	27.0	13.6	4.4	21.5	15.7	4.1
Karnataka	50.4	37.6	37.3	38.7	32.6	33.3
Kerala	39.3	21.1	19.9	23.5	22.3	18.4
Madhya Pradesh	52.8	43.4	43.2	41.3	33.5	34.9
Maharashtra	53.6	42.0	47.1	43.5	38.5	35.4
Orissa	35.9	25.8	26.50	24.5	17.1	21.5

1	9	10	11	12	13	14
Punjab	32.3	10.9	9.8	31.7	19.1	13.4
Rajasthan	63.1	38.3	40.4	55.6	39.7	40.4
Tamil Nadu	51.2	39.4	41.8	41.6	38.3	34.7
Uttar Pradesh	28.1	18.8	17.0	24.6	19.2	18.0
West Bengal	15.5	10.9	10.6	11.7	10.2	10.9

Sources : (i) For Columns 2-5 and 7, Census of India, 1961, 1971 and 1981.

(ii) For Columns 6 and 8, *Sarvekshana*, April 1986

(iii) For Columns 9-14, National Sample Surveys on *Employment and Unemployment in Rural Areas*, Various Issues.

in society as anything but marginal in the economic sphere. Another point that required consideration is that female participation rates are highly correlated to poverty and landlessness in rural India. Given that man is the primary bread winner; women go out to work when their household incomes do not suffice for their basic needs ; more often than not, the poorest households are also the landless. It was observed that, in areas where incomes had gone-up consequent upon the Green Revolution, women tended to withdraw from the labour market due to the improved income effect. Of course, it is also likely that women do not learn new skills and techniques because they are deemed to be primarily engaged in house-work.[10]

However, in the preceding paragraphs we have a bird's eye view of the women's contribution to rural economy in India. The vital role of women in the Indian labour force and their contribution to the national economy has been established beyond doubt. In the subsequent section we will examine women's participation in the developmental programmes.

Women's Participation in Developmental Programmes

India has a surplus labour economy with a high incidence of unemployment and under-employment for both men and women workers, particularly in the country side.[11] The Government of India has been aware of this and has launched a series of specific programmes for women in India. Currently, the Government of India has over twenty seven schemes for women, some women specific and others both for the male and female population.[12] These programmes are being implemented by different Government Departments and Ministries such as Rural Development, Labour, Education, Health, Science and Technology, Welfare, Women and Child Development. The total outlay on the women-specific schemes in the Seventh Plan is 2.4 per cent of the total while a gender break-up of beneficiaries or targets is not available for general schemes (RLEGP, NREP etc.). The government has launched special programmes for providing supplementary nutrition, [illegible] services, health education and other facilities for women.

However, a list of programmes for the development of women and children since independence is presented in Table 3.3.

In almost all the programmes listed in Table 3.3 the major thrust was on the following principal categories :

- Strengthening and improvement of women's work and employment in different sectors of economy,
- Economic rehabilitation of women from the weaker sections of society in the form of training and employment,
- To bring women into mainstream by offering better employment opportunities,
- Providing short stay homes for women and girls with counselling, medical care, psychiatric guidance and treatment and development of skills,
- Preventive and rehabilitative services to women and children and
- To provide general awareness and legal support services.

While the general objectives of development have remained common in all Five-Year Plans, emphasis on specific objectives shifted over the years, keeping in view the national priorities and changing situation. First Five Year Plan emphasized on increased food production, expansion of agricultural inputs, irrigation and power generation got the highest priority. Subsequently, Community Development programme and National Extension Service were introduced (1952) to enthuse people's participation in development Programmes. It was conceived as a multi-dimensional programme, aiming at a process of socio-economic transformation of village life and mobilization of both human and material resources. Initially it had not included any programme for women. In due course women's component under the programme was, however, sought to be provided by the appointment of Social Education Organiser (SEO) to promote women's community participation. The programme that emerged by 1954 was based on the Home Science Extension Approach with the objective of strengthening women's home making roles.

TABLE 3.3

List of Programmes for the Development of Women since Independence

Plan Period	Programmes	Year of Introduction	Implementing Agency/ Department	Coverage	Main Objectives
1	2	3	4	5	6
First Five Year Plan (1951-56)	1. Community Dev. Programme	1952	Distt./C.D. Block/SEO	Complete C.D. Block	Multi-Dimensional/ Mobilization of human and material resources initially not included in any programme for women and child but latter on women component provided by SEO.
	2. Balwadis/Pre-Schools	1952	Voluntary Organisations, KGNMT, ICCW AIWC	Dakshin Murti in Bhavnagar, Vedehi in Surat, Wardha in Maharashtra and some other parts of Western India	Pre-school/Nutrition and Immunisation to children

1	2	3	4	5	6
	3. Women and Childern programme	1952	Department of Child Development	2 to 10 villages	Education/Nutrition and Health Service to target group.
	4. National Extension Service	1953	Child Development Block	—	Almost same as in 1.
	5. Welfare Extension Projects (DP)	1954	CSWB/PIC	About 400 projects of 5 centres each	Home Science Approach.
Second Five Year Plan (1956-61)	6. Welfare Extn. Projects (CD)	1957	CSWB/PIC	About 400 projects of 5 centres each	Women's welfare latter on handed over to Mahila Mandals in 1961-62
	7. Khadi & Village Industries Prog.	1957	KLIC	—	Self-employment for women.
	8. Welfare Extn. Projects (Urban)	1960	CSWB/PIC	40 Projects	As in 6.
	9. Welfare Extn. Centres	1961	CSWB-Managing Committee of Voluntary Organisation	About 1600 centres through 406 Voluntary Organizations	—

1	2	3	4	5	6
Third Five Year Plan (1961-66)	10. Applied Nutrition Prog. (ANP)	1962	Min. of C.D./ Block	1754 Blocks covering 63,318 villages	To provide Nutrition to women and children.
	11. Border Area Project	1963	CSWB/PIC	About 56 Projects with 280 Centres	
	12. Integrated Child Welfare Services Demonstration Projects.	1963	DSW/Block	18 projects	Child Welfare-Health Education etc.
	13. Integrated Pre-school projects	1964	CSWB/PIC	23 Projects	Early/Pre-School Education to children 6 years.
	14. Balwadis in Erstwhile Demonstration Projects.	1965	CSWB/Balwadi Committee	11 Projects 249 Balwadis	
Annual Plan 1966	15. Farmer's Training and Education Programme	1966	—	—	—
Annual Plan 1967	16. Family and Child Welfare Projects	1967	CSWB/Functional Committee	281 Projects of six Centres.	—

1	2	3	4	5	6
	17. Rural Work Programme	1967	—	—	—
Annual Plan 1968	18. Tribal Development Block	1968	—	—	—
Annual Plan 1969	19. Composite Rural Manpower Programme	1969	—	—	—
	20 Programme for women and pre-school children	1969	CSWB/PIC	—	—
Fourth Five Year Plan (1969-74)	21. Balwadi Nutrition Programme	1971	CSWB/Managing Committee of Voluntary Organisations.	5033 Balwadis	To provide nutrition to the target group.
	22. Cash Scheme for Rural Employment	1971	Rural Development/ SFDA/Block	—	—
	23. Small Farmers Development Agency (SFDA)	1972	Rural Development/ SFDA/Block	Blocks	Loan/assistance to small farmers.

1	2	3	4	5	6
	24. Minimum Need Programme (MNP)	1972	—do—	Blocks	To develop basic infrastructure like well, roads, electricity, Health Centre Schools etc.
	25. Special Nutrition Programme (SNP)	1972	DSW/Coordination Committee	69 lakh Beneficiaries	To provide Nutrition to the target group.
Fifth Five Year Plan (1974-79)	26. Creches for the children of ailing working mothers.	1975	DSW/Voluntary Organisations	1385 Units	To provide creche facility for the target group.
	27. Integrated Child Development Services (ICDS)	1975	State DSW/Health/RD/TD/Block	1952 Projects (Till 1988)	1. To improve the nutritional/health status of 0 6 years children 2. Proper psychological physical and special development of child. 3. Reduce mortality, morbidity, malnutrition and drop-out.

1	2	3	4	5	6
					4: effective coordination of policy and implementation 5. Proper nutrition & health education to mother.
28.	Food for work programme	1977	RD/SFDA/Block	Blocks	To provide food for work in rural areas.
29.	Intensive Development Projects	1978	RD/Block	23	—
30.	Social Inputs in Area Development	1978	DSW/RD/Distt/Block	45	To provide Basic facilities to the rural people.
31.	Whole village Development Programme	1979	RD/SFDA/Block	Blocks	—

1	2	3	4	5	6
	32. Training of Rural Youth for Self-employment (TRYSEM)	1979	RD/DRDA/Block	Blocks	Training for self-employment
	33. Integrated Rural Development Programme (IRDP)	1979	RD/DRDA/Block	In all the Blocks/ villages	To provide assistance to below poverty line people to cross the poverty line.
Sixth Five Year Plan (1980-85)	34. National Rural Employment Programme	1980	RD/DRDA/Block	In all the Blocks/ villages	To provide employment to rural poor.
	35. PM's 20 Point Programme	1980	—	—	—
	36. Tamil Nadu Integrated Nutrition Project	1980	State/DSW	One Distt. Six Blocks	To provide Nutrition.
	37. RLEGP	1982	RD/DRDA/Block	All the Blocks/ villages	To provide employment to landless labourers.

1	2	3	4	5	6
	38. Development of Women & Children in Rural Areas (DWCRA)	1983	RD/DRDA/Block	50 Districts	To provide women's employment and income generation activities.
Seventh Five Year Plan (1985-90)	39. Wheat Based Nutrition Programme	1986	Deptt. of Women & Child Development.	3 million beneficiaries in addition to already IIM ICDS	Supplementary Nutrition with a view to cover large number of beneficiaries in tribal, urban slums and backward rural areas.

Sources : Different Plan Documents.

Abbreviations : RD=Rural Development, DSW=Deptt. of Social Welfare, W&CD=Women & Child Development, DRDA=Distt. Rural Development Agency, SFDA=Small Farmers Development Agency, TD=Tribal Development, SEO=Social Education Organisation, CSWB=Central Social Welfare Board.

The programme initiated by the Central Social Welfare Board's Welfare Extension Projects (1954) (Table 3.3) also emphasized on home based activities. The general thrust of this programme was to promote women's groups or organizations at local level through which the programmes for women welfare could be organized.[13] The potential of the Mahila Mandals was sought to be utilized for some selected development and social welfare programmes, such as—Applied Nutrition Programme (ANP), the Integrated Child Development Services (ICDS), and Composite Programme for Women and Pre-school Children.

Two major components of 'Composite Programmes for Women and Children' i.e. Incentive Awards to Mahila Mandals and Training of Associate women workers were introduced during Fourth Five Year Plan. Under the former, mandals showing good performance over a year were awarded cash for undertaking economic projects or activities. The latter was designed to provide orientation to selected women having leadership qualities in organizing village women and assist them in implementing various welfare programmes. During Fifth Five Year Plan a number of programmes have been initiated and more stress was given to promote voluntary action. The objective of these was to utilise the potential of organisations in the implementation of various programmes meant for women and children.

Three major programmes viz. Integrated Child Development Services (ICDS), Social Inputs in Area Development and Development of Women and Children in Rural Areas (DWCRA) were launched specially for women and children during Fifth and Sixth Five Year Plan period. These programmes were jointly sponsored by UNICEF and State governments. The main objectives of these programmes were to provide basic facilities like proper nutrition, health education/services, employment and income generating activities. Another programme called 'Wheat Based Nutrition Programme' was initiated in Seventh Five Year Plan (1986) by the Department of Women and Child Development to provide supplementary nutrition with a view to cover large number of beneficiaries in tribal, urban slums and backward rural areas.

The Seventh Five Year Plan envisaged providing employment to all the unemployed in the rural areas.[14] As a result, 'the Jawahar Rozgar Yojana (JRY), reflect the government's anxiety to give a push to the effort at generating rural employment.[15] This is an employment programme announced in the Budget.[16] It is proposed that a little less than one-third or 30 per cent of employment generated is to be reserved for women in this Yojana. However, it is too early to comment on the success of the JRY, since the programme is yet to reach at the grassroot level.

In most of the development programmes, women as a group have been neglected. Among the various groups of beneficiaries below the poverty line, rural women are most difficult to be reached with assistance. As a result, women are benefiting nominally. According to 1981 figures, out of 20,041 beneficiaries in Rajasthan, only 1,466 were women ; in Tamil Nadu, out of 54,858 beneficiaries 1,873 were women ; and in Gujarat, out of 8,089 beneficiaries 531 were women ; in Uttar Pradesh, out of 26,561 beneficiaries, 1,087 were women (UNICEF, 1982). However, it is clear from the data that a small proportion of women are benefited through developmental programmes.

Summing-up

The proper utilisation of the existing resources, mobilizing the potential resources for use, release of physical and psychic energies of people, improvement and application of skills are most crucial for bringing about change in any society. The process of mobilization is not envisaged properly in most of the programmes. Along with this problem, are the other problems such as lack of political will, lack of committed personnel to work for the emancipation of women, lack of awareness, illiteracy, traditional values and structural constraints etc.

However, an attempt has been made below to indicate the difference in the trends of the programmes in the past and in the current decades.[17]

'Before' (Earlier Programmes)	*'Now' (Thinking Trend)*
— Social Welfare Oriented	— Development oriented
— All women are treated as homogeneous having some responsibilities, needs and problems.	— Accepted women as different in different socio-economic set-ups
— Mainly home makers	— Both home-makers and providers for the family.
— Women's Programme isolated from the main-stream.	— Integration in the major programme for development.
— Oriented to the delivery of services.	— Participatory in nature.

Notwithstanding, much ground needs to be covered yet, to achieve the goal by way of creating an atmosphere of better understanding of the developmental needs for women in the context of national development strategy and a strong infrastructure and other supports to achieve the goal.

In view of the above problems it can be stated that the Panchayati Raj institutions can act as a link between the service agencies at the higher levels and women's group. Such link will be useful in making the different services available speedily and according to local requirements. Panchayats as the bodies at the grass-roots level can create an atmosphere and awareness in respect of women's programmes and their implementation. It will not only result in better appreciation of women's needs but also facilitate their wider participation in the process of development.

REFERENCES

1. Namita Unnikrishnan (1989) : 'How the other half lives', *The Times of India*, March 12, 1989, p. 1.
2. *Ibid.* p. 1.
3. Ashok Kumar (1989) : *Indian Wowen Towards 21st Century*, Criterion Publications, New Delhi, p. 40.
4. Govt. of India (1974) : Report of the Committee on Status of Women

in India, *Towards Equality*, Min. of Education and Social Welfare, p. 101.

5. R.H. Dholakia (1985) : 'On Estimating Women's Contribution to National Product', *Manpower Journal*, Vol. XXI, No. 3, Oct.-Dec., 1985, p. 1.
6. Ashok Kumar (1989) : *Op cit.*, p. 48.
7. Office of the Registrar General, *Census of India*, 1981, Series-I, Paper 3 of 1981, New Delhi.
8. *Ibid*, (see Table 3.1).
9. *Ibid*, (see Table 3.2).
10. Nirmala Banerjee (1985) : 'Women's Work and Discrimination', in Devaki Jain & N. Banerjee's (ed.) *Tyranny of the Household*, New Delhi.
11. Rohini Nayyar (1987) : 'Female Participation Rate in Rural India', *Economic and Political Weekly*, Dec. 19, 1987, p. 2214.
12. Govt. of India (1988) : *National Perspective Plan* 1988-2000 A.D.. of HRD, Deptt. of Women and Child Development, New Delhi, p. xi.
13. S.P. Jain (1981) : 'Promoting Women's Participation in Development Programmes, Role of Govt., Voluntary Organisations and Panchayati Raj', Paper presented in National Seminar on *Role of Women in Rural Development*, organised by NIPCCD & BGMs on Nov. 5-7, 1981, NIRD, Hyderabad, pp, 6-7.
14. Ashok Kumar (1990) : 'The JRY-An Appraisal', in (ed.) of A. Kumar, *Planning, Development and Disparitics*, Common Wealth Pub., New Delhi, p. 235.
15. K.V. Rao (1989) : 'JRY-Old Wine in New Bottle', *Business Standard*, June 21, 1989, p. 5.
16. J.S. Sodhi (1989) : 'JRY-Panacea for Rural Unemployment', *Economic Times*, June 10, 1989.
17. S. Chakravorty (1989) : *Current Programme for Rural Women : The Theme*, New Delhi.

4. MAKINS WOMEN MORE ECONOMICALLY PRODUCTIVE

A.K. Jha

AFTER Independence, it was made obligatory to consider women as a weaker section and the Constitution has guaranteed certain Fundamental Rights and special provisions for protection of women.[1] Several efforts have been made to enhance the status of women from time to time. The integration of women in rural development has been going on since the beginning of the post independence era with varying successes.[2] For the first time, the matter was discussed in Development Commissioners Conference in 195-.[3]

The recent emphasis on the thinking that women can also contribute to the economy of the nation led social scientists, policy makers and administrators to devise ways of developing planned entrepreneurship with reference to women. However, the Government of India is implementing schemes to ensure development of women. The schemes cover a wide ambit such as Rural Development, Labour, Education, Health, Science and Technology, Social Welfare, Women and Child Development etc.

Women's Development During Plans

The First Five Year Plan (1951-56) envisaged welfare measures for women. To spearhead welfare measures, the Central Social Welfare Board (CSWB) was established in 1953 which symbolized the welfare approach to women's problems. The CSWB was also reflective of the community development approach, which envisaged for the first time, the need for organising women into Mahila Mandals or Women's Clubs. A number of studies have shown that the community development (CD) worker, perceived more as a harmonizer of interests rather than a stimulator of awareness, worked closely with the rural elite. Moreover, although rural women came within the purview of the CD programmes, they were not specifically catered to as a target population based on economic or other specific class related criteria. A large majority of poor rural women thus remained untouched.[4]

The Second Five Year Plan (1956-1961) was closely linked with the overall approach to women's issues. The plan recognised the need for the organisation of women as workers. It also perceived the social prejudices/disabilities they suffered. The Plan stated that women should be protected against injurious work, should receive maternity benefits and creches for children. It also suggested speedy implementation of the principle of equal pay for equal work and provision for training to enable women to compete for higher jobs.[5]

The Third Five Year Plan (1961-1966) pin-pointed female education as a major welfare strategy. In social welfare, the largest share was provided for expanding rural welfare services and condensed courses of education. The health programme concentrated mainly on the provision of services for maternal and child welfare, health education, nutrition and family planning.[6]

The Fourth Five Year Plan (1969-1974) continued the emphasis on women's education. The basic policy was to promote women's welfare within the family as the base of operation. The outlay on Family Planning was stepped-up to reduce the birth rate from 40 to 25 per thousand through mass education. High priority was accorded to immunisation of pre-school children and supplementary feeding for children, expectant and nursing mothers.[7]

The Fifth Five Year Plan (1974-1979) emphasized the need to train women in need of income and protection. It also recommended a programme of functional literacy to equip women with skills and knowledge to perform the functions of a housewife (including child-care, nutrition, health-care, home economics etc.).[8]

This Plan coincided with the International Women's Decade and the submission of the Report of the Committee on the Status of Women in India (CSWI). The overall task of the CSWI was to undertake a comprehensive examination of all the questions relating to the rights and status of women in the context of changing social and economic conditions in the country and problems relating to the advancement of women. The report stressed that the dynamics of social change and development had adversely affected a large section of women and had created new imbalances and disparities such as—(i) The declining sex ratio; (ii) Lower expectancy of life; (iii) Higher infant and maternal mortality; (iv) Declining work participation ; (v) Illiteracy ; and (vi) Rising migration.

The CSWI Report led to a debate in Parliament and the emergence of a new consciousness of women as critical inputs for national development rather than as targets for welfare policies. A second significant outcome was the recognition of women as a group adversely affected by the processes of economic transformation. It was realised that Constitutional guarantees of equality would be meaningless and unrealistic unless women's right to economic independence is acknowledged and their training in skills as contributors to the family and the national economy is improved. A major outcome of the CSWI report was the National Plan of Action (1976) that provided the guidelines based on UN's World Plan of Action for women. The National Plan of Action (1976) identified areas of health, family planning, nutrition, education, employment, legislation and social welfare for formulating and implementing action programmes for women and called for planned interventions to improve the conditions of women in India.

An immediate outcome of the National Plan of Action was the setting-up of the Women's Welfare and Development Bureau in 1976 under the Ministry of Social Welfare, to act as a nodal point within the Government of India to coordinate policies and programmes and initiate measures for women's development. The Women's Welfare and Development Bureau was charged with the nodal responsibility of[9]

(a) Coordinating, and collaborating with multifarious programmes in other Central Government Ministries ;
(b) Initiating necessary policies, programmes and measures ;
(c) Collecting data to serve as a clearing house ;
(d) Monitoring programmes for women's welfare ;
(e) Servicing the National Committee on women ;
(f) Follow up on the recommendations of CSWI by formulating proposals and providing guidelines;
(g) Working out financial and physical targets ;
(h) Liaising with multi-national/UN agencies in the field of women's welfare ;
(i) Legal issues and problems concerning women ; and
(j) Implementing programmes and schemes.

In 1977-78 as an exercise for the Sixth Plan, the government appointed the Working Group on Employment of Women. Two other critical reports on village level organisations and participation of women in agriculture and rural development were prepared as part of the exercise. This Plan was undoubtedly influenced by the CSWI Report of 1975. It devoted a whole chapter to Women and Development. For the first time a shift was perceived from welfare to development approaches for women. Influenced by the era that heralded concepts of social justice, the Sixth Plan recognised women's lack of access to resources as a critical factor impeding their development and, among others, the programme providing joint pattas (titles) to men and women was initiated. However, though the plan defined the magnitude of women's problems and suggested development strategies, the 'Family' rather than the 'women' remained the basic unit of development programming.[10]

The Seventh Five Year Plan initiated the concern for equity and empowerment articulated by the International Decade for Women. For the first time, the emphasis was qualitative, focussing on inculcating confidence among women ; generating awareness about their rights and privileges ; and training them for economic activity and employment. In keeping with the spirit of the Decade which aimed at integrating women into mainstream national development, the Plan emphasized the need to open new avenues of work for women and perceived them as a crucial resource for the development of the country.[11]

It was emphasized that technology that causes unemployment or displacement of women must be resisted. Another salient and crucial recognition was the need for organisation of women workers and unionization that could—(a)Make demands for improving legal services to safeguard rights (b) Reduce occupational and health hazards.

While the Seventh Plan did not call for the computation of women's work in these two areas as part of women's contribution to the G.N.P., the identification of these hitherto invisible areas was a significant beginning. Complementing the productive endeavours were the supportive services offered to women, especially maternal and child-care facilities as part of the total package of services for women

The Programmes

The Government of India has over twenty seven schemes for women, some women specific and others both for the male and female population. These schemes are located in different Departments and Ministries of the Government of India such as Rural Development, Labour, Education Health, Science and Technology, Welfare, Women and Child Development, etc. The total outlay on the women-specific schemes in the Seventh Plan is 2.4 per cent of the total while a gender break-up of beneficiaries or targets is not available for general schemes (RLEGP, NREP, etc.)

The Central Social Welfare Board has developmental and welfare programmes for women. The Department also plans a nd executes programmes for women in other Ministries/

Departments. A number of these programmes were envisaged in the Sixth/Seventh Plan periods—viz., Women's Development Corporation, Support to Training and Employment Programme (STEP), Training-cum-Production Centres for Women, Awareness Generation Camps for Rural and Poor Women, Women's Training Centres or Institutes for Rehabilitation of Women in Distress, Short Stay Homes for Women and Girls, Voluntary Action Bureau and Family Counselling Centres, Free Legal Aid and Para Legal Training, Working Women's Hostels etc.

The Community Development Programme in 1952 was a landmark in the history of India and ushered in an era of development with the participation of the people. The Community Development Programme adopted a systematic integrated approach to rural development with a hierarchy of village level workers and block level workers drawn from various fields to enrich rural life. Agriculture, animal husbandry, public health, women's development, rural industries etc. found a special niche in the frame-work cast for this purpose. Five thousand National Extension Service Blocks were created under the Community Development Programmes by the end of the Second Five Year Plan. During the Third Five Year Plan the momentum was maintained through a series of developmental schemes though allocations under the NES programme tapered off. This was succeeded by the Small Farmers Development Agencies followed by Marginal Farmers Development Agencies, Crash Schemes for Rural Employment, Food for Work Programme, Drought Prone Areas Programme and Desert Development Programme in the early seventies. The contents of all these programmes were to strengthen the rural base of the economy, specifically the primary sector comprising agriculture, animal husbandry, etc. and employment through labour intensive works that would create the infrastructure of roads and other community assets for the benefit of the rural people.

Role of Women within the agriculture and rural development strategies in India started with the National Plan of Action (NPA) for women which followed the report of the Committee on the Status of Women in India (CSWI). Subsequently, efforts of women activists, social science institutions and researchers produced enough documentary support to persuade the Sixth Plan document to include a chapter on 'Women and Development' for the first time in the country's history of planned development.

Employment of women has been recognized as the 'critical entry point' for women's integration in mainstream development. The low and deteriorating status of rural women is attributed to their declining economic participation and other factors like the modernisation of the agricultural sector. The need for giving a better deal to the rural women is beginning to be widely recognised. It is now accepted that the participation of women themselves in development activities is the most effective tool for the promotion of the access of women to the benefits of development. A working group set up by the Department of Rural Development, Ministry of Agriculture and Rural Development in 1978 recommended that the major objectives of the development plan for rural women should be-(i) The improvement of their economic status ; and (ii) The promotion of women's organisations to have the collective strength to articulate their needs and promote their participation in the development process.

The Integrated Rural Development Programme initiated in 1978-79 and extended to all the development blocks in the country in 1980-81 was conceived as one of the instruments for a direct attack on poverty. It dealt with individual rural families below the poverty line. Credit from banking institutions and subsidy from the government were given to the families for self-employment and income generation. Under IRDP, a special place was accorded for training rural unemployed youth for employment with the introduction of TRYSEM. An exclusive scheme for the social and economic uplift of women belonging to families below the poverty line. DWCRA (Development of Women and Children in Rural Areas) was launched in 1982 as a sub-component of IRDP.

The specific problems identified concerning rural poor women were—(i) marginality of attention and services to them in rural and agricultural development ; (ii) special constraints that obstruct their access to available assistance and services such as, lack of training to develop their awareness and skills ;

lack of information and lack of bargaining power ; (iii) low productivity and narrow occupational choices ; (iv) low level of participation in decision-making ; (v) inadequate finance and expert guidance for promoting socio-economic activity of rural women and their participation ; (vi) inadequate monitoring of women's participation in different sectors ; (vii) inadequate application of science and technology to remove drudgery ; and (viii) low health and nutrition status.

The National Rural Employment Programme (NREP), assuring wage employment to the unemployed rural population was introduced in 1980. Subsequently, concentration on the rural landless was attempted by the introduction of the Rural Landless Employment Guarantee Programme (RLEGP) in (1983). The Indira Awas Yojana was added as an important component of the programme in the Seventh Plan for constructing houses for SC/STs and freed bonded labourers. Social Forestry was added as another component of the RLEGP with national emphasis on greening, fuel and fodder.

Though women constitute a major work force in agriculture which with regional variation is estimated to be around 60 per cent, thay are invisible in the TV system. Currently there is one major extension programme for women in Karnataka and 2 to 3 such programmes on the anvil in other states. There is an inbuilt resistance observed in them in viewing women within their home making role. Even the visual presentations (slides, filmstrips and films) which are used for the orientation of the functionaries often depict the women in the field and the extension agent talking to the contact farmer on the same field, fail to project the full dimension of women's role.

Non recognition of women in agriculture has many implications. Intensive agriculture and the green revolution have reduced women's participation in on-farm activities but the work load related to the home based farm activities has increased considerably. That has only reduced them from the 'working' to a 'non-working' status. Limited employment opportunities created by technology resulting in the means of production being concentrated in the hands of a few, and increased landlessness for the poor led to men replacing women in many of their traditional areas of employment. But women have had to work and survive. They are thus found gradually moving to the non-traditional sectors seeking employment for survival.

The Department of Rural Development issued directives to the State Governments to give priority to women headed households, enhance the share of women under the anti-poverty programme (IRDP), and the programme of Training for Self-Employment (TRYSEM). Guidelines for NREP and RLEGP envisage increasing participation of women in wage employment and creation of assets specific to the needs of women's groups. At present the share of employment generated under NREP for women is approximately 20 per cent. A special programme for women entitled Development of Women and Children in Rural Areas (DWCRA) was also introduced in 1982, as a sub-component of IRDP to accelerate the process of integration of women in the rural development programmes. Upto 1987, 11,553 groups are reported to have been organised in 106 districts under this scheme.

The scheme of DWCRA could be strengthened and modified in order to ensure that the benefits reach more target groups. The National Rural Employment Programme (NREP) and Rural Landless Employment Guarantee Programme (RLEGP) would generate additional employment to women in the lean season. Under Training of Rural Youth in Self-Employment (TRYSEM), one third of the beneficiaries were expected to be women and special attention was to be given to improve existing skills of women and imparting to them new skills under the programmes of farmers training, fodder production, post-harvest technology, application of pesticide budding and grafting in horticulture, fisheries, poultry, dairy and social forestry etc. The training of women under TRYSEM has exceeded the target to 44 per cent as of January 1988. Out of a total of 37.23 lakh families which received benefits under the IRDP during 1986-87, the number of women-headed families was 5.67 lakhs which amounts to only 15.23 per cent as against the target of 30 per cent. On assessment of the programmes it is observed that considerable efforts are required to elicit the participation of women in these activities.

The training provided under TRYSEM and DWCRA is not always viable and there is a tendency to limit it to a few traditional crafts, though the Department of Rural Development is laying greater stress on taking up innovative activities too. Therefore, a fresh look is needed to be given to identification of trades and activities which may gainfully be taken up by women. Many income generating programmes have not succeeded due to full thought not being given to the input availability, training and marketing of products.

The Accelerated Rural Water Supply Programme (ARWSP) and the Minimum Needs Programme (MNP) are of special significance to rural women who are the victims of drudgery, such as fetching water from distant locations. The Technology Mission on Drinking Water and Related Water Management lays emphasis on purification of water to make it potable, training in the use of water and maintenance of water sources. Women are the target of the awareness creation programmes as well as agents for creating awareness in conservation of water and maintenance of water sources. The low cost sanitation programme is also of great importance to women, who are otherwise subjected to a lot of privation due to lack of appropriate sanitation facilities. Rural Technologies and innovation promoted by CAPART aim at relieving the drudgery to women in several areas of their households and economic activities. They include the improved varieties of stone-grinder, wheel barrow, ball-bearing pulley, groundnut sheller and smokeless chulhas.

The poor performance of the programmes introduced to achieve the integration of women in the development process suggests that only policy directives do not achieve the desired objectives. Programmes do not get implemented due to lack of comprehension of the relevance of women's contribution to national development. Although concern for development of women is well articulated at the central policy making level, an ambivalence is observed at the implementation level. The policy directives issued by the Government of India for the increased share for women in the development programmes and the promotion of a participatory approach, do not provide for corresponding development in the infrastructure, extension, training information support and a strong monitoring system which is particularly lacking at the State level. The programmes for rural women still continue as a separate exercise within the sectoral programmes with marginal attention, resources and inadequate monitoring.

The major short-comings noticed in the implementation of the programmes for women with development objectives are (i) Perpetuation of the concept that women need only welfare services, (ii) That the developmental benefits will automatically accrue to the women as a result of economic development of the family, (iii) Inadequate knowledge and skills for designing socio-economic activities for women and in group organisations, (iv) Lack of supportive services such as credit, child-care, marketing, training and technology for reducing the drudgery.

REFERENCES

1. Ashok Kumar (1989) : *Indian Women Towards 21st Century*, Criterion Publications, New Delhi, p. 5.
2. *Ibid*, p. 5
3. *Ibid*, p. 6
4. Govt. of India (1988) : *National Perspective Plan for Women 1988-2000 A.D.*, Min. of HRD, Deptt. of Women and Child Development New Delhi, p. xiii.
5. *Ibid*, p. ix
6. *Ibid*, p. x
7. *Ibid*, p. 3
8. *Ibid*, p. xiv
9. *Ibid*, p. xiv
10. *Ibid*, p. xiv
1. *Ibid*, p. xiv

5. WOMEN BEYOND THE DOOR STEP

Ashok Kumar

THE status of any given section of population in a society is intimately connected with its economic position which depends on rights, roles and opportunities for participation in economic activities.[1] Economic development is the progress towards an increasingly intricate pattern of labour specialization. The position of women differs in many 'basic features in the community groups. The extant development paradigms had produced a mind-set which saw men as 'producers' and women as 'consumers', assigning men not only the tasks of production but also providing the education and training necessary for the same. Women, on the other hand, were assigned the privileged tasks of familiar nutrition and consumption ignoring their roles as producers. In the World Conference on food and population the women's status was recognised as an important variable in production and reproduction.

While discussing the participation of women in production process, one has to keep in mind the gender role ideology in the mode of production. One line of thinking is to analyse the development of housewife role as a historical product of changes in the economic function of the household and the physical and conceptual separation of domestic work from other kinds of work (Gulati, 1975, Oakley, 1976, Kanther, 1977, Srinivas, 1978). From the second point of view women constitute a labour reserve : being defined first and feremost as domestic workers and may be drawn into the industrial work force or excluded from it according to the needs of capitalist production (Sinha, 1972, Papnek 1973, Bland *et. al.* 1979, Sharma, 1980). Some micro level studies (Gadgil, 1965, Mitra, 1979, Sharma, 1980, Alikhan and Ayesha 1982, Jain, 1983) reveals that women's participation has been declining since 1921. Roasons for the decline of women's participation in the work-force differ in urban and rural areas which are mainly rooted from a strong view that wife's leisure might be taken as a sign of status rather than indigence.[2] The other factors that exhibit women's employment are heavy domestic work-load, lack of assumed work, irregular and under payment of wages, absence of transport facilities, lack of child-care centres and other supportive structures.[3] It is, however, well documanted as well as empirically shown that women are no longer a protected dependent sex in modern India but an active member of this developing nation.

After realising the significant role of women, an attempt has been made in the present exercise on the patterns of women's occupational participation in twenty selected states for which 1981 census is available. The focus is primarily on household and non-household industry occupations and investigated with two-digit occupational classifications. It has also been determined whether women workers are relegated to low status-ranking occupations and how much scope exists for vertical occupational mobility and identified the major occupations in which women workers are in dominance.

II. METHODS OF ANALYSIS

For the purpose of this exercise, the major groups of industry in the Indian Standard Industrial Classification

(ISIC)[4] answering to household[5] and non-heusehold[6], rural and urban are statewise indentified.[7] The idea is to examine specifically the extent of females participation relative to males in the household manufacturing sector, which is usually regarded as the stronghold of female workers. The index of assessing female participation relative to male is to work out the sex ratio (F/M × 1000) of participants in each major groups and study the behaviour of this ratio in household and non-household activity by major groups, rural and urban and different regions.

For the purpose of analysis of variance, a two-way ANOVA test (with one observation per cell) was applied. The mathematical details are as follows :

Let, n_{ij} be the value from the i-th group and j-th region.

The linear mathematical model, i e.,

$$n_{ij} = \mu + \alpha_i + \beta_j + E_{ij} \qquad (1.1)$$

where,

μ is the general mean effect,

α_i is the effect due to i-th group,

β_j is the effect due to j-th region, and

E_{ij} is the error effect due to change,

and,

$$\sum_{i=1}^{k} \alpha_i = O = \sum_{j=1}^{h} \beta_j \qquad (1.2)$$

Null Hypothesis

The null hypothesis is that the groups as well as regions are homogeneous. In other words, the null hypothesis for groups and regions are respectively,

$$H_g : \quad = \quad _2 = \quad \ldots = \quad = 0$$

$$H_z : \beta_i = \beta_2 = \ldots = \quad = 0 \qquad (1.3)$$

i.e., there is insignificant difference between groups as well as between regions,

$$\text{Now, } S_t2 = S_g2 + S_z2 = S_e2 \ldots\ldots \quad (1.4)$$

Where : S_t2=is the total sum of squares.
S_g2=is the S.S. due to Groups.
S_z2=is the S.S. due to regions.
S_e2=is the S.S. due to Error.

For numerical computation of the various sum of squares the following formulas are used.

Total sum of squares=RSS (Row Sum of Squares)

(T.S.S.)—C.F. (Correction Factor)

$$= \sum_i \sum_j nij^2 - \frac{G^2}{N} \quad (1.5)$$

$$\left(\text{C.F.} = \frac{G^2}{N}\right)$$

Where, G is the grand total of all the cell observation and $N = k \times h$ or (rows $\times$ columns)

Groups Sum of Squares

$$\text{(GSS)} = \frac{1}{h} \sum_{i=1}^{k} T_j^2 - \text{C.F.} \quad (1.6)$$

Regions Sum of Squares

$$\text{(ZSS)} = \frac{1}{k} \sum_{i=1}^{h} T_j^2 - \text{C.F.} \quad (1.7)$$

Error Sum of Squares is then calculated by subtracting the total of Group Sum of Squares and Regions Sum of Squares from the Total Sum of Squares.

ANOVA Table for Two-way Classified Data

Source of variation	Sum of Squares (SS)	d.f.	M.S.S.	Variance Ratio
1	2	3	4	5
Groups	$S_g2 = GSS$	(k—1)	$S_g2/(K-1)$	$F_g = \frac{S_g2}{S_E2} \sim F_{(k-1),\ (k-1)\ (h-1)}$
Regions	$S_z2 = ZSS$	(h—1)	$S_z2/(h-1)$	$F_z = \frac{S_z2}{S_E2} \sim F_{(h-1)\ (k-1)\ (h-1)}$
Error	S^2_E	(k—1) × (h—1)	$S_E^2/(k-1)\ (h-1)$	
Total	TSS	(N—1) or (hk—1)		

The degrees of freedom (d.f.) for Groups, Regions and Error should add up to total d.f.

If the observed value of F_g obtained is greater than the tabulated value of F for (k—1), (k—1) (h—1) d.f. at specified level of significance (usually 5% or 1%) then H_g is refuted as that level otherwise it may be retained. Similarly for F_z. If the Error mean Sum of Squares is less than the M.S.S. of any factor of classification then F is calculated by keeping M.S.S. (Error) in the numerator.

In the ANOVA Table, the values of the variance ratio F which are significant at the given level of significance, has been marked with one asterisk (*). Double asterisk (**) represents highly significant value.

Since variance is independent of change of origin, the shifting of origin to some arbitrary point, if necessary, also reduces arithmetic to a great extent.

III. ANALYSIS OF DATA

It is decided to limit the present exercise to the six political regions of India to find out whether significant regional differences exist. Besides, analysis on the basis of all the States and Union Territories would be a very large undertaking. The analysis has been thus confined to variations in the sex ratio participation in rural and urban areas of each of the six political regions distributed by Major Groups of the industrial classification of household and non-household industry.

Ranking of Regions

The first three Major Groups (MG) in order of total number of workers employed in different regions are given in Table 5.1. It is evident from the table that in 4 Regions Major Group-27 (i.e. Manufacture of wood and wood products, furnitures and fixtures) occupies first order followed by Major Group 26 (i.e. Manufacture of Textile Products, other than Footwear).

Non-household industry classification runs through all the 9 Divisions of the Industrial Classification. Among the different Divisions, the Divisions 2 and 3 (Manufacturing and Repair) occupies the first position followed by, Division 9 (Community, Social and Personal services) and Division 6 (wholesale and Retail Trade Hotels). The highest ranking is occupied by Division 2 and 3 for all the regions, followed by Division 9 and 6, although not always in that order in every region.

Ranking of Sex-Ratio of Workers

The sex ratio of workers (i.e. 1000 x Female/Male) other than in cultivation was computed for all industrial major groups. In the ideal circumstances of men and women

TABLE 5.1

A --First-three Major Groups Employed in Household Industry in Different Regions

Region	First order groups	Second order groups	Third order groups
1	2	3	4
India	MG-23 (Manufacture of Cotton Textiles)	MG-27 (Manufacture of wood and wood products, furniture and fixtures)	MG-39 (Repair)
Northern	MG-26 (Manufacture of Textile Products (other than Footwear)	MG-27 (Manufacture of wood and wood products, furniture and fixtures)	MG-39 (Repair)
Central	MG-26 (Manufacture of Textile Products (other than Footwear)	MG-39 (Repair)	MG-27 (Manufacture of wood and wood products, furniture and fixtures.
Eastern	MG-27 (Manufacture of wood and wood products, furniture and fixtures)	MG-23 (Manufacture of Cotton Textiles)	MG-32 (Manufacture of Non-Metallic Mineral Products)
North-Eastern	MG-27 (Manufacure of wood and wood products, furniture and fixtures)	MG-39 (Repair)	MG-23 (Manufacture of Cotton Textiles)

1	2	3	4
Western	MG-27 (Manufacture of wood and wood products, furniture and fixtures)	MG-39 (Repair)	MG-26 (Manufacture of Textile Products (other than Footwear)
Southern	MG-27 (Manufacture of wood and wood products, furniture and fixtures)	MG-39 (Repair)	MG-26 (Manufacture of Textile Products (other than Footwear)

TABLE 5.1

B—First-three Major Groups in Non-household Industry in Different Regions

Region	First order groups	Second order groups	Third order groups
1	2	3	4
India	MG-65 (Retail Trade in Food and Articles, Beverages, Tobacco and Intoxicants)	MG-70 (Land Transport)	MG-90 (Public Admn. and Defence Services)
Northern	MG-70 (Land Transport)	MG-65 (Retail Trade in Food and Food Articles, Beverages, Tobacco and Intoxicants)	MG-02 (Live stock Production)
Central	MG-65 (Retail Trade in Food and Food Articles, Beverages, Tobacco and Intoxicants)	MG-70 (Land Transport)	MG-99 (Services not elsewhere classified)
Eastern	MG-65 (Retail Trade in Food and Food Articles, Beverages, Tobacco and Intoxicants)	MG-90 (Public Admn. and Defence Services)	MG-70 (Land Transport)
North-Eastern	MG-90 (Public Admn. and Defence Services)	MG-65 (Retail Trade in Food and Food Articles, Beverages, Tobacco and Intoxicants	MG-70 (Land Transport)

1	2	3	4
Western	MG-70 (Land Transport)	MG-90 (Public Admn. and Defence Services)	MG-65 (Retail Trade in Food and Food Articles Beverages, Tobacco and Intoxicants)
Southern	MG-65 (Retail Trade in Food and Food Articles Beverages, Tobacco and Intoxicants)	MG-70 (Land Transport)	MG-90 (Public Admn. and Defence Services)

participating equally in every industry or activity, this ratio would be 1000. However, the sex ratio for rural/urban and household and non-household industry has been calculated for all, the Major Groups and are rearranged according to sex ratio category. The consolidated Table 5.2 gives frequency of each of the sex ratio categories. The percentage frequency columns convert the absolute frequencies in the frequency column into percentages, categories I to VI together being taken as 100. The cumulative percentage frequency (to identify the greater-than-type groups) column adds up the percentage frequencies from bottom upwards to the figure 100 in each case.

For household industry in India as a whole, 80 per cent (85% for rural and 80% for urban) of the Major Groups fall in the low frequency category IV (250-499). While in non-household industry this percentage is more than 90 per cent. In other words, the proportion of women employed is less than half of men in more than two-thirds of the Major Groups. This does not bring out the gravity of the situation quite fully. In fact, in one-fifth (20 per cent in rural and 25 per cent in urban) the proportion of women employed is in the very low grading, being as little as between twentieth and a quarter of men employed.

The corresponding picture in non-household industry is much more disturbing, in fact alarming. The maximum participation frequency (34 rural and 36 urban) occurs in the low category V (50 to 249) and 42 per cent of rural and 44 per cent of urban of the Major Groups fall in category VI (Lowest). This means that only in one per cent of the Major Groups in rural non-household industry does the participation of women exceed half of that of men. The great bulk of the rural non-household industry Major Groups have a participation rate of women which varies between a twentieth and a quarter (50-250) of that of men.

As reflected by the sex ratio figures for household and non-household industry, the position of female workers in both rural and urban areas is quite alarming, indeed precarious. Generally speaking, more than 85 per cent of the Major Groups in household and non-household industry,

TABLE 5.2

Percentage Frequency of Participation Sex Ratio in India—Six Regions by Rural and Urban Household and Non-Household Industry, 1987
(Sex Ratio Categorisation : I. Over 1000, II. 750-999, III. 500-749 IV. 250-499, V. 50-249, VI. Below 50)

Category	Rural			Urban		
	Frequency	Percentage Frequency	Cumulative Percentage Frequency	Frequency	Percentage Frequency	Cumulative Percentage Frequency
1	2	3	4	5	6	7
			HOUSEHOLD INDUSTRY INDIA			
I	1	5	100	3	15	100
II	1	5	95	0	0	85
III	1	5	90	1	5	85
IV	8	40	85	3	15	80
V	5	25	45	8	40	65
VI	4	20	20	5	25	25
Total	20	100		20	100	

(Contd.)

1	2	3	4	5	6	7
NON-HOUSEHOLD INDUSTRY INDIA						
I	0	0	100	0	0	100
II	1	1	100	0	0	100
III	0	0	99	2	3	100
IV	7	10	99	2	3	97
V	34	47	89	36	50	94
VI	31	42	42	31	44	44
Total	73	100		73	100	

rural and urban, have sex ratios falling in category IV and below. In other words, not more than 15 per cent of the Major Groups have sex ratios which can be called High, Moderate or Low Moderate, with female participation rates of 500 and above.

IV. ANALYSIS OF RESULTS

An examination of the results in Table 5.3 [analysis of variance dealing with rural household industry workers) shows that there is no significant variation in the number of females per 1000 males between regions. But the variation in sex ratio among Major Groups is significant at 1 per cent level. Statistically speaking, the mean sex ratios for six regions are not quite different from each other. On the other hand, all Major Groups do not have equal mean sex ratio. This inequality of mean sex ratio for all Major Groups having been established, the next obvious question will be to identify the Major Group that has the highest mean sex ratio.

However, Table 5.4 shows the results of analysis of variance for urban household industry work. The results are significant at 1 per cent level, meaning thereby significant variations exist in both Groups as well as regions. Hence, we have not calculated the critical differences for this particular Table whereas for other three tables ranking and critical differences have been worked out. The task there-after will be to rank all other Major Groups by the decreasing mean sex ratio. This is what is done in the first three columns of Table 5.7, with the first column containing the description of the Major Groups of the highest six and the lowest six mean sex ratios.

After ranking the Major Groups, one would like to know whether one Major Group was statistically different from another, that is, to go in for pair-wise comparisons in terms of mean sex ratio. The comparison of one Major Group with another next in rank is done by comparing the mutual mean difference given in the fourth column of Table 5.7 with the computed critical differences given at the bottom of the table.

TABLE 5.3

Analysis of Variance for Rural Household Industry Workers, 1981

Source	Degree of Freedom (DF)	Sum of Squares (SS)	Mean Sum of Squares (MSS)	F-value
Major Group	18	38974794	2165266	28.213 **
Region	5	37160228	7432045	96.83 **
Error	90	6907223	76747	—
Total	113	83042245	—	—

Note : Double Asterisk indicates insignificant at 1% level.

TABLE 5.4

Analysis of Variance for Urban Household Industry Workers, 1981

Source	Pegrce of Freedom (PT)	Sun of Squares (SS)	Mean Seen of Squares (Mss)	F-Volue
Major Group	18	466397038	25910947	1.074*
Region	5	159224271	31844854	1.32*
Error	90	2171957121	24132857	—
Total	113	2797578430	—	—

Note : Single Asterisk indicates significant at 1% level.

The differences in the ranking of regions in rural household industry is presented in the first left hand column in Table 5.7. This shows the significant differences between regions : the North-Eastern commands the highest mean sex ratio followed by Southern, Eastern, Northern, Central and Western respectively. The mean sex ratio for North-Eastern region is significantly different from that of Southern.

Tables 5.5 and 5.6 show that the variance among regions as well as among Major Groups is not significant at 1 per cent level. The ranking of regions presented in the Table 5.7 puts the Southern (in rural non-household industry) North-Eastern (in urban non-household industry) at the top. The ranking of Regions in terms of mean sex ratio, with the qualifying observation that the mean sex ratio for each of them is very low.

Since regions show significant differences, instead of calculating students 't' for different pairs of regions, we calculated the least significant difference at the given level of significance. This least difference is known as the critical difference (CD) and calculated by the formula given below :

$$\sqrt{\frac{2\,S_e^2}{r}} \times t\ 0.05 \text{ for error d.f.} \qquad (1.8)$$

where,

S_e^2 = Mean Sum of Square (M.S.S.)
r = Regions i.e. 6

We arrange the region's mean in their descending order of magnitude. However, the results are presented in the Tables. We therefore, conclude that the difference between mean of North-Eastern region and Southern regions are significantly different from each other since the difference between their mean, viz., 1437 exceeds critical difference i.e., 313.49. All the remaining differences are not significant.

V. FINDINGS

The discussion in this paper is proof of the limited number of industries in which women participate to any significant degree.

TABLE 5.5

Analysis of Variance for Rural Non-household Industry Workers, 1981

Source	Degree of Freedom (DF)	Sum of Squares (SS)SE^2	Mean Sum of squares (MSS)SE^2	F-Value
Major Group	63	5747390	89802	4.79**
Region	5	565605	113121	6.04**
Error	320	7305441	18731	—
Total	389	13618436	—	—

Note : Double Asterisk indicates insignificant at 1% level.

TABLE 5.6

Analysis of Variance for Urban Non-household Industry Workers, 1981

Source	Degree of Freedom (DF)	Sum of Squares (SS)	Mean Sum of Squares (MSS)	F-Value
Major Group	63	7561988	120031	2.65**
Region	5	1212066	242413	5.34**
Error	315	14290799	45367	—
Total	383	23064853	—	—

Note : Double Asterisk indicates insignificant at 1% level.

TABLE 5.7

Ranking of Regions
Rural Household Industry

Region	Mean	Mutual Mean Difference
North-Eastern	1778	1437
Southern	341	84
Eastern	257	23
Northern	234	4
Central	230	39
Western	191	—

Critical Difference (5% Level)=313 .49

Rural Non-Household Industry

Region	Mean	Mutual Mean Difference
Southern	178	6
North-Eastern	172	24
Wastern	148	22
Central	126	19
Eastern	107	39
Northern	68	—

Critical Difference (5% Level)=154.87

Urban Non-Household Industry

Region	Mean	Mutual Mean Difference
North-Eastern	231	77
Southern	154	31
Western	123	45
Norhern	78	1
Eastern	77	2
Central	75	—

Critical Difference (5% level)=241.02

Activities engaging higher rates of female participation in household industry are industries relating to different textiles, tobacco products or forestry and logging which are characterised by high labour intensity and tediousness, less mobility, less skill, coupled with less remuneration. On the other hand, some of the Major Groups in non-household industry are commanding higher rates of female participation. This marked difference in work participation for women in many Major Groups in household industry and several in non-household industry, where higher female participation is invariably characterised by heavy manual labour, drudgery, insanitary conditions of work, and low remuneration, may very possibly have undesirable impacts on society through first, high mortality rate of women (the continuous decline in sex ratio in the population since 1901 is disturbing, to say the least) and, second, through the motivation of increasing the family size to lessen the burden of economic struggle.

REFERENCES

1. Report of the Committee on the Status of Women in India, *Towards Equality*, Govt. of India, Deptt. of Social Welfare, Min. of Education, p. 148.
2. Ashok Kumar (1989): *Indian Women Towards 21st Century*, Criterion Publications, New Delhi, p. 8.
3. *Ibid.* p. 8.
4. The study is based on the 1981 industrial classification. The Indian Standard Classification (ISIC) classifies the industrial distribution of workers into 9 Divisions and 99 Major Groups.
5. Household industry is strictly limited to manufacturing on the household level and excluded manufacturing outside house.
6. Non-household industry, spous manufacturing, construction, trade and commerce, transport, communication and services.
7. Household industry in the Census of India, 1981 is confined to Division 2 and 3 only and the major and minor groups comprising them.

6. WOMEN AS HUMAN RESOURCE : TOWARDS A STRATEGY FOR WOMEN'S DEVELOPMENT IN INDIA

Ashok Kumar & B.L. Sinha

ONE of the greatest asset of our nation is the human resource. About 54 per cent of India's population is in the working age group of 15 to 59 years of age. In this age group are there about 30 million officially registered unemployed persons. Even then we have not formulated any policy to utilise this huge amount of human resources directly.[1] All our earlier policies has been indirectly aimed at employment generation as one of its aim. Even the recently formulated Ministry of Human Resource Development still think in terms of providing education to the rural and urban population and how to improve the skills of the teachers.[2] This may solve the problem in future only and that too if a proper coordination takes place among various departments and the ministries. Why not the Ministry come out boldly on this issue ? Let there be a policy which can say that those below secondary education should serve in the army compulsorily for a period of ten years and those completed secondary education for five years and so on.[3] Needless, to about those who have not stepped into the schools and about the dropouts. Even in the advanced countries such as USA, and Germany this system exists, particularly for higher level posts in the government. When we can copy all the other things from the West, why not this too ? What prevents us from doing this ?

However, for any kind of developmental activities one has to take of the availability of resources. The proper utilisation of resources are the most important aspects of planning. In this context, we have to take stock of the resources according to the types of résources. The following Fig. 6.1 shows the types of resources which required indepth study :

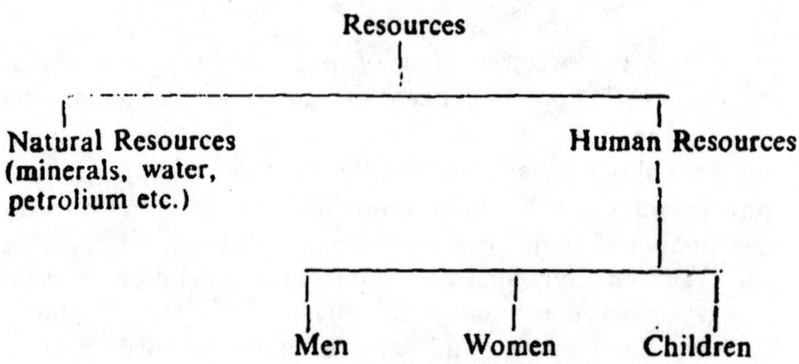

Fig. 6.1

The above figure exhibits different types of resources taken into account for any sorts of developmental activities. However, in the present exercise we will discuss about the women resources only.

Women as Human Resource

In India, a high priority has been accorded to achieving economic development. Most of the developmental programmes and projects stress on an increase in national production. They squarely deal with fundamental issues of human equality, social justice, human resource development, etc. The development of the human potential by creating a better quality of human beings has not been substantially emphasised. Women development has remained all the more neglected. They have not been given the status of equality in the society. They are subjected to ill-treatment, socio-economic injustice, exploitation and physical and mental torture.

Women constitute about 50 per cent of the population. Statistically speaking (1981) out of total literate population of 36.1 per cent, the percentage of literate males was nearly 47 per cent and the percentage of literate female was 25 per cent. This shows that the disparity in the literacy rate between males and females is very wide. Figures of women's employment are very important indicators of the fact that the participation of women in the total work force of the country is actually decreasing. In 20 years of planning, the female population has increased by 15 per cent (9 million). There has been a 7 per cent fall in women's employment between 1961 and 1981.[4] These statistical figures of women's employment are very important for the determination of women's status. The decline in the female participation in the total workforce over the past 30 years could be directly described to other factors which affect women adversly. One, there has been a fall in the female population compared with the male population. Two, there is an increasing gap between the male and female literacy rates in India, And three, the participation of the women in the decision-making body is declining.

However, in spite of these depressing statistics it is also to be noted that though in terms of quantity the participation of women in the total labour force is declining in terms of quality, the diversity of occupations of which women can enter and are willing to enter irrespective of the traditionally or unconventiality of the occupations, is showing an upward trend

Several programmes have been formulated and implemented, but they have hardly changed employment status of women. What is more important is that a women needs freedom not from her own womanhood but from the centuries old shackles of injustice and discrimination. For improving the status and to bring women into the mainstream women needs economic independence. Not to be a burden on anyone can give a woman immense self-confidence. Secondly, she needs a different kind of education and grooming. Thirdly, she needs to have an access to medical and health facilities. Fourthly, social evils like child marriage, child labour, *purdah system*, *sati pratha*, and dowry which stand in the way of women's development should be removed. Fifthly, the attitude of women themselves has to be shaped to creative and positive thinking.

Strategies for Women's Development

Some strategies are to be viewed holistically and not as isolated piecemeal actions. In order to be truly effective, the overall employment strategy for women should be viewed as a package comprising employment opportunities, legal safeguards, training support and social services, awareness generation and mobilisation Only then will a purposeful synergy be achieved.[5] The corrective strategies are broadly addressed to the factors which have been reviewed earlier as constraints. Those strategies must aim to create new avenues for employment of women, upgrade their existing employment conditions as well as productivity and employment potential, make them a more articulate and conscious workforce, and assure them better status and recognition as workers.

Employment

The employment potential for women is likely to grow very slowly in the organised sector. On the other hand, there is a considerable scope for employment in the agricultural and service sectors. Diversification in agriculture and in the other major sectors of rural employment offers enormous potential for employment. Horticulture, commercial vegetable growing, food processing, fisheries and poultry, agro-industry offer ample opportunities to rural women. Unemployed young women could be trained in extension work for importing the necessary skills in these activities. Besides, a variety of new occupations could be created for women workers in the areas of agro-based industry weaving, textile printing, ready-made garments, production of stationery and preparation of indigenous herbal medicines and packaging etc.[6]

The service sector in the rural areas is a need and reality offering scope for local women to be absorbed with the minimum training being provided. Nurseries, creches and *anganwadis* also offer employment opportunities for a large number of women. The areas of simple health care like immunization, diagnostic screening (testing of blood etc.) and other health functions could be opened to intermediary levels without affecting the overall standards. These facilities are not currently available to poor families particularly in the rural areas. Middle level workers could be trained for employment in the provision of these services.[7]

There is an immediate need to diversify the prevailing occupational base so as to promote skilled employment on a wider scale. Currently, training is imparted in traditional occupations like carpentry, welding, smithing, tailoring, book binding etc. which is also male oriented. It is now necessary to provide training to women in such non-traditional fields as well. An area based identification of potential occupational clusters would have to be undertaken systematically in different regions of the country in order to determine the nature and size of opportunities that could be made available.

Effective linkages between metropolitan and large urban areas with the surrounding hinterlands is another modality with considerable potential for employment generation. The demand from these urban and metropolitan centres in the fields of food processing, packaging, transportation, storage and other services could open up large areas for production, processing and marketing, thereby providing employment opportunities in such areas on a sizeable scale.

Expansion of small scale industries is widely recognised as a means of creating potential for employment. Suitable institutional mechanisms for the promotion of small scale industry need to be developed to assist in the provision of credit, supply of raw materials, organization of marketing and creation of skills necessary for these enterprises. Two of the important areas requiring urgent attention for the expansion of cottage industries are—(i) Upgradation of skills in order to raise the status of workers to that of artisans and improve the quality of products (ii) Education, training and organizations of workers for collective action on various issues.

Appropriate technologies and modernization of their occupations would have to be inducted to increase their income potential. The role of middlemen who have been getting sizeable benefits disproportionate to their investment and efforts has to be reduced. Producer Cooperatives are one such strategy to reduce dependance.

An appraisal is necessary to examine the viability/marketability of the trades for which training and assistance is being provided by the government. The Central Social Welfare Board (CSWB) is implementing some employment generation schemes under which voluntary agencies in the country have been availing of financial assistance. Training is also given under TRYSEM etc. and socio-economic schemes are undertaken under DWCRA, IRDP and the Training-cum-production scheme of the Department of Women and Child Development, etc. An attempt should be made to expand the categories to encompass new and viable trades and create necessary linkages.[8]

Training

A systematic human resource development strategy focused on women is essential. Three levels of training are envisaged, viz. (i) The grass-roots level ; (ii) The middle level ; and (iii) The policy and planning level. The content of a training strategy should encompass five principal components as follows :[9]

—Organisational and extension training ;
—Skill training ;
—Management and entrepreneurial training ;
—Sensitization of administrators/implementors to women in development issues ; and
—Training of trainers.

Components of training is to be geared to functionaries, catalysts, extension workers at the grass-roots, middle and supervisory level personnel, teachers, organizers of cooperatives, etc. It should aim at conscientization on legislation, environmental health, nutrition and sanitation, education functional literacy, paralegal training and related aspects. Effective group mobilization, communication skills, skills needed for organization and management will be emphasized in this training alongwith functional knowledge. Particular attention will be paid to the attitudinal/behavioural component essential for reaching programmes women at the grass-roots.

Skill Training

Refers to skill training with special emphasis on the nine major sectors of women's employment i.e. agriculture, dairying, fisheries, small animal husbandry, khadi and village industries, handlooms, handicrafts, sericulture and social forestry. This type of training will entail upgrading existing skills in these areas as well as training of women in appropriate technologies. It will be aimed at programme beneficiaries as well as catalysts/functionaries, extension and supervisory workers. These skills need to be imparted on the widest scale to rural women in order to encourage them to achieve household self-sufficiency as well as supplementary income. Also included will be the skill training in the urban/modern sector with regard to assembly, manufacturing and processing for larger industries as well as small scale firms. Wherever possible women's employability has to be increased in the organised sector as the employment conditions in the unorganized sector indicate the need for a shift in the occupational structure. In generating such skills, care will be taken to ensure that the training imparted does not push women into sectors where mobility is limited, wages are low, health hazards are high and worker benefits are not enforced.

Managment training refers to training in project formulation, monitoring, evaluation, information systems, credit/marketing management, and other skills required to administer and manage projects, as well as supervisory and entrepreneurial skills. Such training could be provided with the help of technical institutes (ITIs, Polytechnics, etc.) where special courses for training of women workers and entrepreneurs could be started. In conducting such courses, banks, voluntary organisations, and private and public sector industries could be effectively utilized to help formulate viable entrepreneurial projects for the trainees. Special training programmes to promote rural entrepreneurship in particular would need to be designed.

Training should seek to achieve sensitization of bureaucrats to the critical need to integrate women in development. The objective will be to develop appropriate attitudes and knowledge for planning/monitoring/implementing programmes and policies for women. Such training needs to be imparted through the training programmes of the Department of Personnel as well as other governmental and non-governmental agencies. A particular emphasis in this category of training must be to train the officers in charge of enforcement machinneries at the Central and State levels, workers of quasi-governmental bodies, and voluntary agencies. The Womens Division at NIPCCD is already undertaking sensitization programmes for police officers/judiciary to the issue of crimes against women.

In view of the criticality of training for the development of women, setting up of a National Resource Centre for Women is imperative. By playing a coordinating/interventionist role it would identify and strengthen existing governmental and non-governmental agencies to carry out training policy and programme research and information dissemination. The Resource-Centre-would provide a new thrust for training and work towards translating national developmental goals into a systematic grid of programmes and schemes for training in skills/knowledge/attitudes at different levels. As a preparatory step, it would be essential to identify and classify the various types of training institutions in the country. Examples of such institutions[9] are agriculture and rural home science centres ; schools of social services, khadi and village industries, as well as vocational training centres ; universities, ITIs, polytechnics, agriculture and veterinary schools, engineering colleges, krishi vigyan kendras, etc. At present, they have no special focus on training only for women, but these should take up new courses under a coordinated effort, monitored, and planned by the resource centre. In addition, newly established training and extension departments, as well as existing training institutions, agencies, management bodies, and grass-roots organizations should be involved in imparting training to women.

Once women are able to rise above the stereotyped roles assigned to them, they can contribute in achieving the goals of development, i e. increasing the nation's GNP and per capita income, providing health for all by A.D. 2000, fulfilling the educational targets, etc. To achieve this, it is essential to provide a climate suitable for development of women. Isolated micro-level reforms would be a meaningless exercise in this context.

REFERENCES

1. N. Shridharan (1989): 'Whither Democratic Planning: Some Issues', in edited book of Ashok Kumar aud R.P. Mamgain, *Manpower Planning in India*, Criterion Publications, New Delhi, p. 29.
2. *Ibid*, p. 2a
3. *Ibid*, p. 30
4. Sushma Sapru (1989) : 'Socio-economic Status of Women : Problems and Perspectives', in edited book of R.K. Sapru, *Women and Development*, Ashish Publishing House, New Delhi, p. 235.
5. Govt, of India (1988) : *National Perspective Plan for Women 1983-2000 A.D.*, Min. of HRD, Deptt. of Women & Child Development, New Delhi, p. 5.
6. *Ibid*, p. 31
7. *Ibid*, p. 31
8. *Ibid*, p. 32
9. An exhaustive National Directory of such training institutions has been compiled by the women's division at NIPCCD.

7. ROLE OF ICDS IN WOMEN'S DEVELOPMENT

Ashok Kumar

INDIA'S developmental efforts, through successive Five Year Plans, have contributed a great deal towards commendable improvements in the health indices of the country. As a result of these efforts the death rate is now one third of what it was in 1921, and the life expectancy has gone up from 24 years in or around 1901 to about 52 years in 1981.[1] Successive Five Year Plans have laid special emphasis on providing at least minimum health facilities integrated with family welfare and nutrition for women and children, side by side with the acceleration of women's education. The Sixth Plan has not only continued but expanded the maternal and child health schemes including ante-natal, natal and post-natal services. The nutritional status of child at birth is influenced by the nutritional status of his mother. 'It is well documented' as the Sixth Plan says, 'that a vast majority of pregnant and nursing mothers, especially belonging to the low socio-economic group, live on diets which are inadequate'. The high incidence of pre-maturity, low birth weight of babies and neo-natal mortality can be attributed to poor nutritional conditions among the mothers.[2]

Considering the above problems, the scheme of ICDS was launched in 33 projects on experimental basis in October 1975. Encouraged by the evaluation of the programmes by the Programme Evaluation Organisation (PEO) of the Planning Commission and the All India Institute of Medical Sciences. The concept and the performance of the programme over the years had attracted wide attention not only in India but abroad too. However, several studies have been conducted on the impact of services delivered through ICDS projects. The Planning Commission conducted a Baseline survey of the ICDS Projects for the reference period of 1976-77 to find out the state of preparedness of these projects to deliver the services effectively and whether necessary infrastructural support was available for that. The Repeat Round was undertaken of the projects for the reference period of 1977-78 to evaluate the extent of coverage of target population and the impact of the scheme on beneficiaries.[3]

The research studies conducted on ICDS observed that the scheme helped, by and large, in improving the health and nutritional status of children and mothers in the target groups. On the other side, it was observed that the concept of pre-school education was not correctly understood by the ICDS functionaries, the component of health and nutrition education has not received adequate attention ; and the community contribution and participation in the ICDS programme was negligible. Lack of effective supervision of the programme at the *Anganwadi* Level for functional coordination at different levels of the project, and lack of involvement of local leadership in the programmes were identified as some of the operational constraints in the effective implementation of the ICDS Scheme.[4]

Effective delivery of services under the ICDS scheme depends to a large extent on the organisational system designed for providing the services and on the utilisation or management of inputs available for them. Again, the functioning of an organisation is not merely dependent on the internal structural arrangements but also on the external factors and environment—social, political and economic. However, ideally the organisational system might have been designed to deliver the services, its effectiveness will equally depend upon the attitudes of the people in general and the target groups in particular, and the commitment of local leadership to the objectives of the project. Similarly, effective use of resources for achieving the project objectives will mostly depend upon the leadership. The administrative procedures prescribed by the government provide broad guidelines to implement a project, but the achievement of its objectives will depend to a greater extent on the project incharge and his/her managerial abilities and skills in harnessing the human and material resources for the project and utilising them.

Women in India have too much of work, too little food combined with too many pregnancies. In addition majority of our women have too large a share of responsibility for the family well-being and too small a share in the decision which affect it. Considering the major role played by women our government has been actively implementing, improving and expanding a most ambitious and comprehensive plan to increase the survival rate and enhance the health, nutrition and learning opportunities of children and mothers. This plan, 'The Integrated Child Development Services (ICDS)'—is India's gift to her own future—her own children and their mothers.

The Scheme

An ICDS scheme was launched in 1975 for providing opportunities of physical and psycho-social development to children in the age-group of 0-6 years through an integrated package of early childhood services.[5] These services include supplementary nutrition, immunisation, health check-up, referral service and treatment for minor illness for these children and expectant and nursing mothers, pre-school education for children in the age group of 3-6 years, and nutrition and health education for all women in the age group of 15-45 years. The services are provided through the ICDS projects located mostly at the Block level. With its expansion in successive Five Year Plans, ICDS is today a major programme of child development at the national level with the following main objectives :

(i) to improve the nutritional and health status of children in the age-group of 0-6 years ;

(ii) to lay the foundation for proper psychological, physical and social development of the child ;

(iii) to reduce the incidence of mortality, malnutrition and school dropout ;

(iv) to achieve effective coordination of policy and implementation amongst the various departments to promote child development ; and

(v) to enhance the capability of the mother to look after the normal health and nutritional needs of the child through proper nutrition and health education.[6]

The objectives are sought to be achieved by delivery on integrated package of early childhood services comprising supplementary nutrition, immunisation, health check-up and referral services for children (0-6) and for expectant and nursing mothers ; by providing health and nutrition education to mother ; and by imparting non-formal pre-school education to the children in the age group of 3-6 years.[7]

The objectives of the scheme are implemented through the projects located at the block level.[8] Launched initially with 33 ICDS projects on 2nd October 1975 on experimental basis in 22 States and the Union Territory of Delhi, the scheme covered 1644 projects by the end of March 1987.

II

At the district level, the District Development Commissioner (DDC) who is a senior officer of the IAS cadre, Deputy Director, Social Welfare, (posted at the Commissionary level) and District Welfare Officer at the district level is responsible for coordination of programmes under the scheme. The Health Department being the nodal department for the implementation of ICDS projects, the CDPO and the Supervisors who are on the regular cadre sometimes treated as on deputation while Bihar, unlike in many states, where Deputy Collectors (selected through State Public Service Commission) are being posted as CDPO. Another significant aspect of the system is that the DDC (a senior IAS officer equivalent to Collector in Status) exercises overall administrative control, and thus, facilitating coordination and cooperation among the officers concerned with ICDS at the district and project levels.

III

District Saharsa has been bifurcated from the old Bhagalpur district in 1954. Three sub-divisions viz. Saharsa proper, Supaul and Virpur and 16 blocks constitute the district. It is located in the North-eastern part of India from 26° 34" to 25° 27" latitude and 86° 12" to 87° 80" longitude.

The ICDS project Mahisi (which is a block also) is situated 18 kms. north of Saharsa which is one of the most backward blocks of the district with a literacy rate of per cent (as per the 1981 Census). The population of the project area was 95,154 (48640 male and 46514 female) in 1981, out of which 20,370 belonged to Scheduled Castes. Though the project was identified as a rural one, 79 out of 81 villages (per cent) were inhabited.

A detail block profile of the selected block Mahisi (Saharsa) is given in Table 7.1. The project area was mainly inhabited by Hindus with agriculture as their main occupation. There were also large section of Muslim inhabitants. Wells and handpumps were the main source of drinking water in the project village. In about 30 per cent of the villages, the drinking water was considered not safe as open wells were the main source of water supply. Diarrhoeal diseases and malaria were reportedly common in the area. The project had a total number of 95 Anganwadi Centres (covering 79 villages)

TABLE 7.1

Block Profile—Mahisi (Saharsa)

(As per 1981 Census)

Items	Number	Percentage
A. Total Number of Villages		
(a) Inhabited	79	—
(b) Uninhabited	2	—
B. Area (in sq. kms.)	222.9	—
C. Populaton (1981)—Total	95,154	—
Male	48,640	51.11
Female	46,514	49.89
D. Literacy (1981) — Total	17,572	18.46
Male	14,028	14.74
Female	3,544	3.72
E. Scheduled Caste— Total	20,370	21.40
Male	10,434	51.22
Female	9,936	48.77
F. Work Force		
(i) Total Main Workers	33,078	34.76
(a) Cultivators	13,361	40.39
(b) Agricultural Workers	17,976	54.34
(c) Workers engaged in household industry, construction and repair works.	254	0.76
(d) Other workers	1,487	4.49
(ii) Marginal workers	3,533	3.71
(iii) Non-workers	58,543	61.52
G. (a) Registered Birth (1979)	675	—
(b) Registered Death (1979)	257	—

grouped under five sectors with a supervisor incharge of each sector.

However, Panchayats were functioning in the project villages. There were no Mahila Mandals and youth clubs in the project areas.

(b) Village Profile

A brief profile of the selected *Anganwadi* villages is presented in Table 7.2. The 10 Anganwadi villages under study has a population varying between 960 to 1250. A close perusal of the table reveals that villages dominated by Scheduled Castes population are having very less infrastructural facilities. Whereas villages of high castes are having all the facilities. Most of the (7 out of 10) were connected by transport. Hand-pumps and wells were the main sources of drinking water in most of the villages. The villages falling in 'diara' land of river Kosi, however, had problems of drinking water due to scattered nature of houses. The villagers had to walk long distances to fetch water.

Out of 10 only 2 villages had high school, 4 had middle school and 6 had primary school. The health infrastructure in the project covered one PHC at Mahisi, the block head-quarters, and sub-centres at different places. However, only 4 sample villages were having this facilities in the village itself and remaining villages were located five to 12 kms. away from the sub centre (Table 7.2).

Although State of Bihar has a strong system of *Panchayati Raj* but involvement of *Panchayats* in the project area was almost nil except helping functionaries in providing accommodation to AWCs. The villages under study had no Mahila Mandals nor any Yuvak Mandal.

In the Minimum Needs Programme (MNP) and also in Rural Electrification Programmes (REC), there is a provision to provide electricity to the scheduled castes villages on priority basis. But out of 10 villages under study five villages were dominated by scheduled castes and none of them were electrified. However, based on this brief village profile it can be inferred that scheduled castes and other backward communities are still lagging behind as far as availing of government developmental efforts are concerned.

The Anganwadi Workers

Among the 95 Anganwadi Workers of the project area, a little more than one-fifth 21 or 22.10 per cent belonged to the Scheduled Castes community. Population-wise five out of

TABLE 7.2
Profile of the Selected Anganwadi Villages under the ICDS Project, Mahisi District Saharsa, Bihar

Items	Teghara	Ramsala	Maina	Baluwaha	Belshi
1	2	3	4	5	6
1. Population—Total	1065	1015	1000	1250	1075
S.C.	1065	—	960	—	300
O.B.C.	—	215	40	345	775
2. School —High	—	yes	—	—	—
Middle	—	yes	—	yes	—
Primary	—	yes	yes	yes	yes
3. Whether connected by transport	yes	yes	no	yes	yes
4. Road to AWC (K=Kutcha, P=Pucca)	—	P	K	K	P
5. Whether had sub-centre (Y=Yes, N=No)	N	Y	N	Y	N
6. If sub-centre is not located, distance from the nearest one (in kms.)	5	—	8	—	5
7. Whether electricity is there or not ?	no	yes	no	yes	yes
8. Drinking water facilities	yes	yes	no	no	no

Table 7.2 (Contd.)

Items	Arräpatti	Telwa	Jalai	Lahuwa	Rajanpur
1	7	8	9	10	11
1. Population—Total	1125	1025	1100	1175	960
S.C.	425	1025	1100	900	—
O.B.C.	200	—	—	275	60
2. School —High	—	—	—	—	yes
Middle	yes	—	—	—	yes
Primary	yes	—	—	—	yes
3. Whether connected by transport	yes	no	no	yes	yes
4. Read to AWC (K=Kutcha, P=Pucca)	P	K	K	K	P
5. Whether had sub-centre (Y=Yes, N=No)	Y	N	N	N	Y
6. If sub-centre is not located, distance from the nearest one (in kms.)	—	8	10	12	—
7. Whether electricity is there or not ?	yes	no	no	no	yes
8. Drinking water facilities	yes	no	no	no	yes

Source : Field Survey.

the 10 selected villages under sample were predominantly inhabited by the Scheduled Castes. However, this did not coincide with the fact that five of the 10 Anganwadi Workers who belonged to the Scheduled Castes were coming from the same villages where the Scheduled Castes population was high. Notwithstanding, in two villages where the SC population was predominent, the Anganwadi Workers did not belong to the SC community.

A brief profile of Anganwadi Workers is presented in Table 7.3, which exhibit that more than one-third or 36.86 per cent workers belonged OBC (Other Backward Castes) category followed by SC (22.10 per cent) and Hindu low castes. Hindu high castes and Muslim community had the equal share i.e. 10.52 per cent, as far as caste-wise representation of Anganwadi Workers is concerned.

Age structure of Anganwadi Workers was biased towards young. Majority of the Anganwadi Workers (45 or 47 per cent) were in age group of 21-25 years followed by 26 30 years (35 or 36.84 per cent). About 16 per cent workers were in the age group of 31 and above and none of the workers were from the age group of 15-20.

As far as educational structure of the Anganwadi Workers is concerned, a little less than two-third or 62.12 per cent were educated upto middle only. About 36 per cent were below high school standard and only 2.10 per cent had crossed this bar. However, none of them were illiterate. A total of 91 underwent job training for the Anganwadi Workers and four were untrained. Their experience as Anganwadi Workers varied from less than one year to more than 5 years. Majority of them (35 or 36.85 per cent) were having more 5 years experience.

Eight out of 10 Anganwadi Workers were local (staying in the same village where their respective Anganwadi Centres were located) and rest two were coming from the neighbouring villages situated at a distance of one to 5 kilometers. The details regarding this are as follows :

TABLE 7.3

Profile of Anganwadi Workers

Variables	No. of AWWs	Percentage
Age : 15-20 years	0	0.00
21-25 years	45	47.38
26-30 years	35	36.84
31 & above	15	15.78
Total	95	100.00
Caste : S.C.	21	22.10
S.T.	0	0.00
Sub-total	21	22.10
Other Backward Caste	35	36.86
Hindu High Caste	10	10.52
Hindu Low Caste	19	20.00
Muslim	10	10.52
Others	10	10·52
Total :	84	100.00
Education : Up to Middle	59	62.12
Below High School	34	35.78
High School & above	2	2.10
Illiterate	—	—
Total	95	100.00
Work	4	4.21
Experience : Less than 1 year		
1-3 years	24	25.26
3-5 years	32	33.68
5 years plus	35	36.85
Total	95	100.00
Training ; Trained	95	95.78
Untrained	4	4.21
Total	99	100.00

Sources : ICDS Project, Mahisi, Saharsa.

	Numbers
Local	8
Non-Local (coming from a distance of 1-2 kms.)	1
Non-local (coming from a distance of 3-5 kms.)	1
Total :	10

Functioning of Anganwadi Centres

Time devoted by the Anganwadi Workers on different activities and informations regarding functioning of the Centres were also collected. The services provided under the project included supplementary nutrition for children in the age group of 0·6 years and pregnant and nursing mothers, health check-up, immunisation and referral services for them, health and nutrition education for mothers and non-formal pre-school education for children in the group of 3·6 years. The Anganwadis, the focal points for the delivery of services under ICDS, were functioning from 10.00 a.m. to 2.00 p.m. with the following schedule of activities :

Time devoted by AWCs	*Activity*
10.00 a.m. to 11.00 a.m.	Bringing of children to the AWC by the Helper
11.00 a.m. to 1.00 p.m.	Pre-school activity
1.00 p.m. to 1.30 p.m.	Washing of hands and face of children.
1.30 p.m. to 2.00 p.m.	Distribution of supplementary food.

However, it was observed during field visit that in almost all the selected Anganwadi Centres, the above mentioned programme schedule was followed except washing of hands and face of children. The programme schedule given above was broad and flexible in the sense that the Anganwadi Workers could adjust it keeping in view the local situation and take initiative in conducting the activities in a more interesting and effective manner. On the whole, it was observed that the

Anganwadi Workers were not giving proper attention in washing of hands and face of children.

III

The beneficiaries under the ICDS Scheme are categorised under expectant mother, nursing mothers, children (6 months to 3 years) and children (3 years to 6 years). However, under those categories number selected for supplementary nutrition and number of children registered for pre-school education in the complete ICDS project area were also selected and given in the table 7.4 below :

TABLE 7.4

Number of Beneficiaries under the ICDS Project

Category of Beneficiaries	No. Selected for SNP	Percentage	Children registered for PSE
Expectant mothers	570	1.225 (6.03)	—
Nursing mothers	570	1.225 (6.03)	—
Children (6 months-3 yrs.)	4,507	(47.70)	—
Children (3-6 years)	3,800	(40.22)	3,800
Total :	9,447	9.92	3,800

Source : ICDS Project Mahusi, Saharsa (Bihar)

Note : Figures in bracket are the vertical percentage.

Above Table7.4 shows that only 9,447 or 9.92 per cent of the total population were the ICDS beneficiaries for SNP in the block. As far as expectant and nursing mothers are concerned they were having equal share i e. 1.225 percent. Among the total beneficiaries, children below 3 years (6 months to 3 years) were having good share i.e. 47.70 per cent. The corresponding figures for children of 3 years to 6 years was 40.22 per cent. A total of 3800 children in the ICDS project area were registered f or pre-school education.

It was observed during the field visit to the selected Anganwadi Centres that the attendance of children was very low. Only 10-20 children were present in majority of the Anganwadi Centre (6 out of 10) for both the programmes. The number was less than 10 in one Anganwadi Centre. However, a detail information regarding this is presented in Table 7.5.

TABLE 7.5

Attendance of Children at the Anganwadi Centres

No. of Children	No. of AWCs showing attendance of Children	
	As per Register	During visit
31—40	3	0
21—30	5	3
10—20	2	6
Less than 10	0	1
Total :	10	10

The number of children was more in three of the Anganwadi Centres, where the pre-school activity in an innovative way, was going on. In none of the Centres more than 30 children were seen though the number of children enrolled at various centres varied from 15 to 60 and 20 to 50 for children in the age groups of 6 months to 3 years and 3 to 6 years respectively.

Having noticed the poor attendance of children at the Anganwadi Centres, the reasons thereof were also identified, from both parents as well as Anganwadi Workers, which are as follows :

— At the time of field visit, supplementary nutrition was suspended due to interruption in food supplies (State Food Corporation);

— At some places children were not interested in having *Khichudi* only. And through out the year they were given *Khichudi* as supplementary nutrition.

— The community were not properly educated about the ICDS programme. Because in PSE activities they were expecting something else and so not found it worthwhile to send their children to Anganwadi Centres;

— In the villages predominent by higher castes, parents preferred to send their children to school than Anganwadi Centres (even 3 years of children);
— In the Scheduled Castes families, older children had to stay back at home to look after their younger siblings while both the parents went out for work;
— It was also complained by the villagers that Centre used to remain closed for longer period (10-15 days) in a month so they found it not worthwhile to send their children; and
— This problem was also discussed by the ICDS functionaries. As per their statement children will only come to the centre when supplementary nutrition will be provided to them. Interruption in food supply leads to the poor attendance of children at the Anganwadi Centres.

Supplementary Nutrition

Under the programme, supplementary nutrition food was used to be served (not regularly) to the children and the pregnant and lactating mothers. Mostly they were given *Khichudi* of of rice and *dal*, which were locally available. However, the Anganwadi Workers were expected to see that the children wash their hands before the food under SNP was served to them. Though this was the practice at most of the Anganwadi Centres, the children observed were by and large untidy. The Anganwadi Workers found fault with the parents for not keeping their children neat and clean. It was, however, observed that no effort was made by the Anganwadi Workers to keep the children clean. The children were sent back home as they were at the end of the Anganwadi Programmes. If the Anganwadi Workers sent them neat and tidy, it would give the parents a feeling that children are developing good habits while attending the Anganwadi Centres.

Most of the parents reported that they were sending their children regularly to the Anganwadi Centres, but it was observed that many of them were not doing so particularly when supplementary food could not be served due to delay in supplies This was more so with the parents of the SCs community for whom the main attraction at the Anganwadi

Centres was the food that was distributed. At one of the Centres it was observed that not even a single beneficiary was present.

The timing of food distribution was found not suitable, it being afternoon by that time, the parents were expecting a full meal for their children and therefore, they had a feeling that the quantity of the food given was not sufficient.

As far as pregnant and nursing mothers are concerned, very few of them were going to the Anganwadi Centres for taking their share of supplementary nutrition food. Some of them felt it below their dignity to go to the Anganwadi Centre just to have a little share of food while others did not find time to go there as they were busy in their fields or household work. It was also observed that not many women were aware that supplementary nutritions food was provided to pregnant and nursing mothers through the Anganwadi Centres. They were not educated properly about the service available at the Anganwadi Centre.

By and large, the Anganwadi Workers were not getting any help from the beneficiary mothers in running the Centre. They were only coming sometimes to leave their children at the Centre and take them back at the end of the Anganwadi activities, as they used to keep themselves busy in own household/agricultural work. They were of the view that the Anganwadi Workers, does not require their help as she was provided with Helper to assist her. They, however, expressed their willingness to help Anganwadi Worker, if at all she required any help from them. These observations suggest that the mothers were not clear on how they could participate in the Anganwadi activities. It could be that the Anganwadi Workers were not clear that how they could involve mothers in conducting the programmes of they did not like to involve them.

Food supplies under SNP to the Centres were generally irregular (as per the responses of both the workers and local people) and their quality unsatisfactory. It was also reported that worm-infested food material was supplied on one or two occasions. As reported by the ICDS functionaries, the community people were not at all in a position to contribute anything being very poor any affected by natural calamities like drought, floods (Koshi river) etc. in the case of Anganwadi Centres not approachable by road, the village people were not helping the Anganwadi Worker by picking up the supplies from the roadside and delivering them to the Centre.

However, supplies of food material for SNP and medicines to the Anganwadi Centres were not regular as reported by the Anganwadi Workers. Four out of 10 Anganwadi Centres studies had inadequate facilities for storage of supplies. The articles in these Centres were kept at a neighbouring house to avoid theft. All the Anganwadi Centres were provided at the beginning with very few utensils/equipments for running the programmes, one-third of the Anganwadi Workers felt that certain items like bucket, rope, plates and spoons should also be provided at the Centre.

Pre-school Education

The next important activity of the programme is the pre-school education (PSE) with having the following main objectives[9] :

— developing adequate muscular coordination and basic motor skills in the children ;
— developing creativity and aesthetic appreciation and elementary hygienic sense :
— providing opportunity for interacting with other children of the same age-group ;
— developing in the child the ability express his thoughts and feelings influent, correct and clear speech ; and
— developing the habits of attending the AWC regularly.

The programme content of pre-school activity is, therefore, centred on play activities as "play is the main activity by which child learns and develops". These play activities should be based on indigenous material and culture.

However, in the project under the pre-school activity was being conducted generally from 11 a.m. to 1.00 p.m. The activity, starting with a prayer, included recitation of nursery rhymes, teaching of numbers and narration of stories. It was observed that Anganwadi Workers were not having sufficient kit materials to perform this activity. Many of the Anganwadi Workers were of the view that the play material became unusable and required replacement.

In most of the centres, the children were asked to recite the same old prayers, poems, and tell the same old stories narrated to them when the project started functioning. However, the workers were making efforts to involve children in outdoor games. They were trying to develop the concept of number, shape, colour, size, etc. But it was observed that almost in all the centres those activities were repeatitive. Thus, the pre-school activity, although conducted regularly, were repeatitive and monotonous and not attractive enough for the majority of the Anganwadi Centres. It was also unattractive for them as the same old charts and play material provided when the project started functioning were used for these activities.

Health and Nutrition Education

Health and nutrition education to the target groups were mainly given by the Female Health Worker (FHW)/ANM, Multipurpose Health Worker, Anganwadi Worker and LHV as mentioned by the beneficiaries. Under this component ANMs were supposed to motivate the people for adoption of family planning practices and were supposed to educate them on the need to get their children immunised and keeping their surroundings clean.

It was however, observed that very few were imparting health and nutrition education to the people. Very few of the Health Functionaries make the visit of their alloted areas/villages as reported by the villagers.

Health Check-up, Immunisation and Referral Services

As in the case of health and nutrition education, these three activities are also the main responsibility of the Primary Health Centre (PHC) and its dispensaries and sub-centres. In the project there was no regular health check-up at the Anganwadi Centre. The Medical Officer (MO) was conducting an overall health check of children to identify infectious diseases etc. when, immunisation services were provided through mass campaigns,

Although weighing scales were available at each Anganwadi Centres but the weights of children were not taken as per the schedule. Growth charts and Health Cards were distributed to AWCs long back when the project started. It was also observed during the field visit that the mothers were usually not present when the weights of their children were taken at the Anganwadi Centre except in the case of those who were in the age-group of 6 months to 2 years. However, the mothers should be required to be present when the weights of their children were taken irrespective of their age-group as they could help Anganwadi Worker in taking the weights. Their presence would also help in creating health awareness among them.

As regards immunisation, services were being provided for mothers and children through the sub-centres. The children of Anganwadi Centres were usually immunised twice in a year against different diseases. The targets and achievements of the complete area of the PHC is given in the Table 7.6.

It is evident from Table 7.6 that for none of the items achievements are more than fifty per cent. This problem was discussed with staff posted at PHC level. As per their statement the poor achievement is because of the lack of man power at both the level ; field as well as PHC/dispensaries. However, supply of vaccines and medicines for each items are adequate.

So far as the referral services are concerned, services were not provided in a regular and systematic manner. The FHWs/MPWs on their visits to villagers, advised the parents of children suffering from typhoid, dehydration etc. requiring special attention to go to the nearest dispensing centre or PHC or district hospital as the case may be. But there was no regular follow-up of such an advice as there was no formal referral service system at the project through a referral card or slip. There were no referral services or regular follow-up even in the case of malnourished children.

TABLE 7.6

Targets and Achievements under different items of PHC Mahisi, Saharsa (Bihar) 1989-90

Item	Target	Achievements	Percentage
D.P.T.	3950	1820	40.07
D.T.	3900	1630	41.79
B.C.G.	4077	895	21.95
Polio	4077	1685	41.32
T.T.	5233	1925	36.78
Vitamin 'A'	—	75 Bottles	—
Iron Tabs. (Children)	—	88,00	—
Iron & Folic Acid Tablets for women	—	78,000	—
Simple Drugs	—	Adequate	—

Sources : PHC, Mahisi.

Very few people were approaching the sub-centre for treatment of minor ailment though they were aware of the facility available there. The beneficiaries however, by and large unaware of the referral services due to the reason that these were not effectively provided. Similarly, they were not aware that the health check-up of children and mothers was a part of the services delivered through the Anganwadi Centre as it was not done regularly.

The opinion of parents varied in regard to the benefits received from the services rendered through the AWC. Most of them (60%) felt that their children benefited from the SNP. Next in order were the immunisation and pre-school services (65%). Only about one-third of them mentioned that their children benefitted from the service of health check-up. None of them were aware of the referral services provided through the AWC.

Most of the parents particularly those belonging to the scheduled castes community, could not, however, spell out how the services benefitted their children. Only a few of them specified the benefits received as follows :

Services	Bene fitted	Not benefi-tted	Don't Know	Total
S.N.P.	12(60%)	4(20%)	4 (20%)	20(100)
P.S.E.	13(65%)	7(35%)	—	20(100)
Health Check-up	7(35%)	—	13(65%)	20(100)
Referral Services	—	—	20(100)	20(100)

— they learnt good manners ;
— developed school going habit ; and
— learnt the correct usage of words etc.

Visits of Functionaries to the Anganwadi Centres

For proper functioning of the Centre, the Anganwadi Workers required the guidance and Supervisors. It is, therefore, the information regarding visits of different functionaries (their frequency) to the AWCs were also collected and presented in the Table 6.7.

TABLE 6.7

Visits of Functionaries to AWCs During 1989

Frequency	Functionaries visited			No. of AWCs	
	CDPO	MO	Supervisor	ANM	LHV
2-5 times	6	8	3	7	9
6-9 times	2	1	3	3	1
10-14 times	2	—	2	—	—
Total	10	9	8	10	10

The above Table 6.7 reveals that the Supervisor (ICDS) most frequently make visit of the Anganwadi Centres. Five out of

10 studied centres have reported that ICDS Supervisor had made visit of their Centres more than six times. High frequency of visit was followed by the CDPO. The Anganwadi Workers said that their Supervisors helped them in solving some of the problems. They persuaded the parents to send their children regularly to the Anganwadi Centre. They explained different columns in the registers/reports and guided the workers in filling the required information, etc.

Coordination at Different Levels

As the ICDS scheme adopts an inter-sectoral approach involving more than one department or agency of the Government, panchayats and voluntary agencies, there is all the more need for coordination of their efforts in delivering the package of services for children and mothers. Coordination will help maximum utilisation of the available resources The scheme provides for formal mechanisms through the Constitution of coordination committees at the state, district and project levels.

It was observed that at the district-level there was no coordination committee formally constituted. However, the DDC/DHO and Deputy Director Social Welfare holds periodic review meetings with the health and non-health functionaries. At the block/project level, BDO/Pramukh (elected Chairman) at the Block is the Chairman and CDPO is the Convenor of the Committee. The project level committee is expected to meet on 28th of every month. It was however, observed that the meetings of the committee were not convened regularly. The project level meeting was generally attended by MO, CDPO, LHV, ANMs and Supervisors. But as the minutes of these meetings were not available in the office of CDPO, it was not possible to find out specifically what problems were discussed there. However, as reported by the CDPO, getting the accommodation for AWCs and getting articles from the SFC etc. were some of the problems discussed in the last meeting.

On the whole, it was observed that at the block level BDO, CDPO and MO were having good coordination between each other but at the grass-root level coordination between the health functionaries and AWWs were not so.

Community Participation

The community participation in the effective implementation of the programme is a very important aspect which cannot be ignored. For the purpose of present study, representatives of Panchayat, village leaders and influential persons of the village were considered. The primary-school teacher who is usually a source of information and an agent for creating community awareness was also included under the category of leaders.

A total of 20 community leaders were interviewed However, their observations may only indicate the general trend. Most of them said that they were visiting the Anganwadi Centre twice a month and some of them stated almost every alternate day. The functionaries who consulted them mainly included the CDPO, Supervisors, AWWs and ANMs. They sought the advice of the leaders on various matters like improving the attendance of children at the AWCs, creating community awareness about the programme.

However, by and large, it was observed that the community participation was poor in programme implementation. None of the Anganwadi Centre's building was donated by the community. Neither they were helping the functionaries in repairing the same. The conditions of all the visited centres were very poor. The AWWs used to keep the articles in nearby houses. During field visit *Mukhia* of the village panchayat was also consulted in this regard and few of them were agreed upon it and giving assurance that under the *Jawahar Rozgar Yojana* they are going to construct the building for Anganwadi Centre.

IV

SUGGESTIONS & RECOMMENDATIONS

(a) About Proper Functioning

(i) The primary school teacher or one of the fellow villagers or elders or local persons should supervise/guide the helper in the distribution of supplementary nutrition food when the Anganwadi workers are on leave or even in normal course also ;

(ii) The local people should help the Anganwadi Worker in procuring the articles for Anganwadi Centre ;

(iii) For running the Anganwadi Centres more effectively in regard to programme and activities, role of functionaries, supplies and equipments, support and participation of the beneficiaries and the village panchayats should also be enhanced.

(iv) The community should be made more aware of the activities and programmes of the Anganwadi Centres ;

(v) The priority should be given to the local girls for recruitment of Anganwadi Workers so that she can put more efforts in running the Centre ;

(vi) The Supervisors and the CDPO should make frequent visits to the Anganwadi Centres and provide necessary guidance to the Anganwadi Workers ; and

(vii) The Anganwadi Centres should be provided with adequate number of utensils and containers for storage of food material.

Different Components of the Scheme

(i) Supplementary Nutrition Food supplies under SNP by the State Food Corporation were very irregular and their quality were unsatisfactory. It was reported that worm-infested food material was also supplied on one or two occasions. Hence, it is suggested that the food supplies should be regular and of a better quality ;

(ii) There should be variety in the supplementary food given to mothers and children ;

(iii) When there is delay in food supply community should contribute the locally available food for the Anganwadi Centre ; and

(iv) It was suggested by the parents that children may also be given sweets and biscuits sometimes in place *Khichudi*.

Pre-school Education

(i) It was observed that pre-school activity, although conducted regularly, were repeatitive and monotonous and not attractive enough for the children. It was also unattractive for them as the same old charts and play material provided when the project started functioning. Hence, it is suggested that some more teaching materials through the help of UNICEF should be supplied.

(ii) Parents were in the opined that Anganwadi Worker should give more emphasis on teaching numbers and alphabets to children. Thus, in this regard parents need to be educated by the functionaries about the concept of pre-school education ; and

(iii) Toys may be provided or should be prepared by the AWWs/Community through waste materials for children at the Anganwadi Centre to attract and educate them simultaneously.

Health and Nutrition Education

(i) Under this, the ANMs/FHWs were motivating the people only for adoption of family planning practices to achieve their targets. They should also give emphasis on the need to get their children immunised and keeping their surroundings clean;

(ii) Very few of the Anganwadi Workers were imparting health and nutrition education during their home visit. But they should use puppets and posters to educate the community on the evils of alcholism, drug addiction etc. through group meetings of the beneficiaries.

Health Check-up, Immunisation and Referral Services

(i) The mothers should be required to be present when the weights of their children were taken irrespective of their age-group as they could help the Anganwadi Worker in taking the weights. Their presence would also help in creating health awareness among them;

(ii) The health functionaries working at the grass-root level (like, ANM/FHW, LHV or MPW) should make regular visit at least twice in a month for health check-up and once in six months for immunisation;

(iii) Local people had a feeling that the Anganwadi Centre is only to look after the children, so at least the ANM should be provided the required medicines during home visits;

(iv) Long back when the project was started a medicine kit box was supplied to the Anganwadi Workers through UNICEF after that neither any medicine nor tool kits were given to the workers. It is, therefore, suggested that atleast first-aid medicine should be supplied at the Centre; and

(v) Referral services, were not provided in a regular and systematic manner. The beneficiaries by and large, were unaware of the referral services due to the fact that these were not effectively provided. However, grass-root level health functionaries should be given special attention and advised the parents to go to the nearest dispensing centre or PHC or district hospital as the case may be.

REFERENCES

1. *Manual on ICDS*, (1984) : NIPCCD, New Delhi, p. 4.
2. *Ibid*, p. 4.
3. L.S.N. Murthy & Sunita Mathur (1988) : *Project Management : A Study of ICDS Projects*, NIPCCD, New Delhi, p. 7.
4. *Ibid*. p. 7.
5. *Ibid*. p. 1.
6. India, Ministry of Social Welfare, *Integrated Child Development Services Scheme*; (Revised), New Delhi, 1982, p. 2-3.
7. Murthy & Mathur (1988), *op. cit.* p. 4.
8. The block is an administrative unit covering about 100 villages with an average population of one lakh.
9. Murthy & Mathur (1988) *op. cit.*, p. 27.

3 WOMEN IN POLITICS : WHAT MAKES A DIFFERENCE

Ashok Kumar

I

MINIMALLY, a political perspective requires that some activity called "politics" be differentiated from other activities, relationships, and patterns of action. If all conceptual boundaries are blurred and all distinctions between public and private are eliminated, no politics can exist by definition. The relatively open-textured quality of politics means that innovative and revolutionary thinkers are those who declare politics to exist where politics was not thought to exist before.[1] Should their reclassifications stick over time the meaning of politics-indeed of human life itself—may be transformed. Altered social conditions may also provoke a reassessment of old, and recognition of new, "political" realities. However, the theme of political participation of women has raised a major dilemma. On the one hand, it is the fundamental right of every citizen to contribute to the decision-making process. It is, in fact, the citizen's duty as well and is based on the presumption that each member has adequate means and conditions to achieve a full realisation of his personality as an entity in society. On the other hand, from a feminist perspective, an analysis of women's participation in political processes has questioned the narrow definition of political participation as accepted by mainstream of political scientists and policy-makers.

Political participation can be considered to include an involvement in any form of organised activity that affects, or seeks to affect, these power relationships. It refers broadly also to "activities by those not formally empowered to make decisions, these activities being mainly intended to influence the attitudes and behaviour of those who have powers for decision-making".[2] Infact, protests and demonstrations against those in power also form part of political participation. Women's participation has covered a range of activities including movements, protests and support meetings on all issues connected with labour, dowry, rape, demestic violence, price-rise, food adulteration and deforestation, as also movements for the promotion of peace.

But however, with particular reference to women's participation in India has only been limited application, mainly because of various dubious considerations of social, economic and political variables. Broadly, political participation of women is severely limited due to a nexus of traditional factors, these are the domination of Indian politics by considerations of caste, class, religion, feudal and family status etc., all of which are parochial essentially patriarchal forces that work in favour of men against women. Consequently, women are still left on the periphery of the political process, and political participation remains elusive to most of them, inspite of their voting and election and also capture of some seats of power and influence.

As amply brought out by various scholars, the most crucial problem in any attempt to measure women's political participation simply by studying official or organisational membership and voting, is the finding that much of the Third World politics occurs outside conventional political institutions.

Hence, political participation seeks also to reorganise the lives of members of human society, and ensure that the participation by women is not under-estimated by being branded 'non-political' and women's concerns treated as 'social' in nature.[3]

There are several socio-economic constraints by which women have been marginalised. The number of women in leadership positions at the local, village, district and national level is still not commensurate with their numbers in society. In India, limited adult franchise was granted to women in 1937. Since then, women have been participating in political processes, as voters, as candidates contesting the elections, involved in deliberations both in the State Assemblies and Parliament and also through holding public office at different levels in the judiciary.

II

Voting is the basic activity by which the citizen get assimilated in the political process.[4] Women's participation in formal elections is to a great extent dependent on the mobilisation efforts of the political parties, general awareness among the community of the importance of exercising franchise, and the overall political culture. Table 8.1 below shows the participation of women in the elections :

TABLE 8.1

Year	Total Voting %age	% turnout of new voters	% turnout of women voters	No. of women elected
1977	60.49	65.63	54.96	19
1980	56.92	62.15	51.22	28
1984	63.61	68.17	58.60	43
1989	DNA	DNA	DNA	28

If we have a look at the past history of the women's political participation we find that no serious efforts appears to have been made to mobilise women as a political pressure group by any political party. Caste, personality and families of candidates appear to be more important to voters than party ideology or affiliations. Some other factors like education, religion, class and tradition also seem to affect women's participation. However, voting as an indication of political participation for women in India, has its own strength and weakness. Voting has a tremendous impact for equalising and mobilising women. Yet, it has to be noted that voting requires the least initiative and internal motivation. Very often the woman citizen treats the day of voting as a welcome break from her dull and tiring routine and does not appear to have a notion of why she should vote for a particular candidate.

However, over the years, the number of women contestants in parliamentary elections has not increased. Political parties seem uniformly reluctant to field women candidates. The high cost of electioneering is another deterrent to most women candidates. Because of these factors there is an increasing tendency among women to contest elections as independent candidates (Table 8.2).

The proportion of seats won by women to the Lok Sabha stands in 1988 at 46 seats out of a house of 537 seats. The Rajya Sabha has 28 women in a house of 245 seats. There has been a greater representation of women in Rajya Sabha by nomination.[5] The pattern is not ve y different at State level (Table 8.3). The all India total stands at 44 women elected out of 241 women contestants, as against 1486 men out of ?415 male contestants. For instance, in Orissa 1980, for the House of 147 members, 10 contestants were women of whom only 5 were elected. In 1980 in Tamil Nadu, 5 out of 17 women candidates won. An indepth study of women of grass-roots level politics reflects a similar trend. However, the redeeming factor is that women in rural areas are capable of progressive thinking and have the potential for viable social participation if a conscious effort is made to secure their involvement.

Women in 9th Lok Sabha (1989)

Luck apparently ran out for the majority of women who tried their electoral fortunes for the ninth Lok Sabha as only 28 of approximately 150 women candidates in the fray have been returned. This poor presence of women in the House of 525 at the moment gives a clear indication that the new Lok

TABLE 8.2

Women Candidates put up by Political Parties for Elections to the Lok Sabha

Year	Congress-I		Congress		C.P.I.		C.P.I. (M)		Swatantra		Janta
	No. of Conte-stants	No. of Succe-ssful Cand.	No. of Conte-stants	No. of Succe-ssful Cand.	No. of Conte-stants	No. of Succe-ssful Cand.	No. of Conte-stants	No. of Succe-ssful Cand.	No. of Conte-stants	No. of Succe-ssful Cand.	No. of Conte-stants
1957	—	—	26	23	4	2	—	—	—	—	—
1962	—	—	33	27	2	2	—	—	9	5	—
1967	—	—	33	23	3	—	1	1	2	2	—
1971	21	15	14	—	3	1	2	1	2	1	—
1972	22	6	—	—	3	1	2	2	—	—	15
1980	32	20	10	—	2	1	3	2	—	—	20
1984	39	36	—	—	2	1	3	1	—	—	4
1989*	53	15	—	—	1	1	—	2	—	—	—

			Janata Dal		Others			Independents		
Year	No. of Successful Cand.	No. of Contestants	No. of Successful Cand.	No. of Contestants	No. of Successful Cand.	No. of Contestants	No. of Successful Cand.	No. of Contestants	No. of Successful Cand.	Per cent
1957	—	7	—	—	—	5	2	42	27	5.4
1962	—	8	—	—	—	13	—	65	34	6.7
1967	—	10	3	—	—	13	2	62	31	5.9
1971	—	29	1	—	—	11	3	82	22	4.2
1972	8	24	—	—	—	4	2	70	19	3.4
1980	2	60	—	—	—	15	3	142	28	5.1
1984	—	96	1	—	—	20	3	140	42	8.1
1989*	—	—	—	—	2	—	—	—	—	—

Note : Blank columns indicate either the party was not in existance or data was not available.
**THE HINDU*, New Delhi, December 7, 1989 P. 6.

TABLE 8.3

No. of Candidates Constitution elected to the State Legislative Assemblies by Sex in States UTs from 1978-83

Sl. No.	State/Union Territory	1978 Contested M	1978 Contested F	1978 M	1979-80 Elected F	1979-80 M	1979-80 Contested F
1	2	3	4	5	6	7	8
1.	Andhra Pradesh	1491	47	284	10	—	—
2.	Assam	917	21	125	1	—	—
3.	Bihar	—	—	—	—	2925	77
4.	Gujarat	—	—	—	—	950	24
5.	Haryana	—	—	—	—	—	—
6.	Himachal Pradesh	—	—	—	—	—	—
7.	Jammu & Kashmir	—	—	—	—	—	—
8.	Karnataka	1137	28	215	9	—	—
9.	Kerala	—	—	—	—	589	13
10.	Madhya Pradesh	—	—	—	—	1950	50
11.	Maharashtra	1777	42	280	8	1488	49
12.	Manipur	—	—	—	—	394	7
13.	Meghalaya	255	7	59	1	—	—

1	2	3	4	5	6	7	8
14.	Nagaland	—	—	—	—	—	—
15.	Orissa	—	—	—	—	720	10
16.	Punjab	—	—	—	—	703	19
17.	Rajasthan	—	—	—	—	1375	31
18.	Sikkim	—	—	—	—	233	11
19.	Tamil Nadu	—	—	—	—	1012	17
20.	Uttar Pradesh	—	—	—	—	4525	94
21.	Tripura	—	—	—	—	—	—
22.	West Bengal	—	—	—	—	—	—
23.	Andaman & Nicobar Islands	—	—	—	—	—	—
24.	Arunachal Pradesh	84	2	30	—	93	2
25.	Chandigarh	—	—	—	—	—	—
25.	Dadra & Nagar Haveli	—	—	—	—	—	—
27.	Delhi	—	—	—	—	—	—
28.	Goa, Daman & Diu	—	—	—	—	174	3
29.	Lakshadweep	—	—	—	—	—	—
30.	Mizoram	153	1	29	1	147	3
31.	Pondicherry	—	—	—	—	128	4
	Total	5814	148	1022	30	17406	420

	1979-80		1982-83			
	Elected		Contested		Elected	
	M	F	M	F	M	F
1	9	10	11	12	13	14
1. Andhra Pradesh	—	—	1647	73	282	12
2. Assam	—	—	448	3	108	1
3. Bihar	312	12	—	—	—	—
4. Gujarat	178	5	—	—	—	—
5. Haryana	—	—	1068	27	83	7
6. Himachal Pradesh	—	—	432	9	65	3
7. Jammu & Kashmir	—	—	505	7	75	—
8. Karnataka	—	—	1327	38	222	2
9. Kerala	135	5	682	17	136	4
10. Madhya Pradesh	302	18	—	—	—	—
11. Maharashtra	269	19	—	—	—	—
12. Manipur	60	—	—	—	—	—
13. Meghalaya	—	—	309	8	60	—
14. Nagaland	—	—	244	1	60	—
15. Orissa	142	5	—	—	—	—
16. Punjab	111	6	—	—	—	—
17. Rajasthan	190	10	—	—	—	—
18. Sikkim	32	—	—	—	—	—

1	2	9	10	11	12	13	14
19.	Tamil Nadu	229	5	—	—	—	—
20.	Uttar Pradesh	401	24	—	—	—	—
21.	Tripura	—	—	119	11	56	4
22.	West Bengal	—	—	1179	26	287	7
23.	Andaman & Nicober Islands	—	—	—	—	—	—
27.	Arunachal Pradesh	29	1	—	—	—	—
25.	Chandigarh	—	—	—	—	—	—
26.	Dadra & Nagar Haveli	—	—	—	—	—	—
27.	Delh	—	—	379	12	52	4
28.	Goa, Daman & Diu	30	—	—	—	—	—
29.	Lakshadweep	—	—	—	—	—	—
30.	Mizoram	29	1	—	—	—	—
31.	Pondicherry	29	1	—	—	—	—
	Total	2478	112	8415	241	1486	44

M - Males
F - Females
Source : Election Commission of India, New Delhi.

Sabha is lacking much of the colour and glamour of the previous one which had 43 member of the fair sex, most of them on the treasury benches. The women parliamentarians, however, constituted less than eight per cent of the Lok Sabha's total strength. This percentage has dropped to about five in the just constituted ninth Lok Sabha.

Incidently, of the 28 women members, almost half are the new faces. It is a mere coincedence that the number of women returned this time is just the same as it was in 1967 as well as 1980. This number dropped to 21 in 1971 and declined further to 19 in 1977. It went up to 28 in 1980 and swelled to 43 in 1984. Significantly, the majority of the women returned to the Lok Sabha in 1984 belonged to the Congress party but this time the case was reverse.[6]

Encouraged by the spectacular success of its women nominees in 1984 the Congress (I) decided to field 53 women candidates this time but unfortunately most of them could not withstand the anti-Congress (I) wave that swept the northern region and fell at the hustings. Of the 53 women put up by the Congress (I), only 15 got elected, representing a success rate of 28 per cent. The BJP which put up 10 women candidates had a better showing with five of them being returned. The performance of the Janata Dal and the other parties including the Leftists has not been any better with two women each entering the Lok Sabha under the banner of the JD, CPI (M) and Akali Dal (Mann group). The CPI and the BSP have one each.

The scenario, therefore, is that of the 28 women in the House, 26 is adorning the opposition benches while two of them on the treasury side. Of the 12 women nominated by the Congress(I) in Uttar Pradesh only three were elected. However, the high profile women MPs have been rejected by the electorate. Among those defeated were also the close relatives of politicians in power. Bihar returned two women this time against nine in 1984. Of the 10 women fielded by the Congress (I) in State only one emerged victorious. The other member is Janata Dal's. Andhra Pradesh improved its tally returning all the five Congress (I) women nominees. Similarly, Punjab improved its tally by returning three women. Madhya Pradesh also returned three women. Tamil Nadu also retained its tally by returning both of the Congress (I) MPs. West Bengal which had sent five women to the Lok Sabha in 1984 has returned just two this time. Surprisingly, no women candidate has been returned from Orissa, Gujarat, Haryana, Himachal Pradesh, Jammu and Kashmir, Delhi, Arunachal Pradesh, Sikkim, Tripura, Meghalaya and Nagaland.

As far as political parties are concerned, although at election time declarations are made of granting 15-20 per cent seats to women, no party has been able to achieve the target. In many studies have shown that before the women's decade, political parties were not even stressing on women's issues, in their campaigns or mobilising rallies. In the last decade all political parties have shown great interest in women's problems as a result of various developments but primarily due to the pressure of women's groups. Parties in their manifestos promise to women all opportunities for increased participation in social, economic and political life. Yet the record of most of the parties is poor so far as women are concerned.

However, a number of political parties have strong women's wings spread all over the country, but advocate revival of traditional values, encourage fundamentalism, eulogise mythological women characters and generate communal sentiments. Some others struggle around issues such as economic demands, world peace, atrocities against women, secularism, national integration, price-rise etc.

III

Women's participation in trade unions has been a topic which has acquired significance during the last two or three decades. Studies have shown that though it might be difficult to participate in day-to-day activities of the trade unions, women have provided very great strength during crisis periods, such as strikes. A distressing fact is that the prevalence of partiality prevents men colleagues from accepting women's crucial role.

Today after more than a decade of our struggle we find to our satisfaction that the question and problems of working women and women in general are being discussed widely in our country by various organisations, individuals, press and also by the Government. The question is also being highlighted in international forums. Despite these efforts, many trade unions in the country are yet to pay adequate attention to women's issues and joint efforts have to be made to make a common cause to fight for the demands of working women. A recent report also gives the picture of the women membership in the CITU and the proportion of women office bearers in some of the states. The total membership has been around 10 per cent in 1986, and an infinitesimal proportion as office bearers.

It is well known that women constitute a majority of the unorganised labour force. The working conditions in this sector are abysmal. There is no security of jobs, no fair wages, no facilities and no rights to demand for the improvement of their situation, etc. It goes to the credit of grass-roots level organisations such as the WWF and SEWA and the researchers who have highlighted the problems of these women.

Informal Participation

Of course, more strikingly, mass participation of women was recognised during Civil Disobedience Movement in 1930 and also during the Quit India Movement of 1942, when thousands of women courted arrest. Women from various castes, communities and regions have participated voluntarily and together, to raise their voice on important issues. Current rural struggles in Bihar, Himachal Pradesh, Marathwada region and five Tamil Nadu districts centre on various issues ranging from expropriation and redistribution of the land of a Bodhgaya mahant in Bihar, the politics of liquor licencing and government water supply in Himachal Pradesh, to struggle for canal water and public lands by untouchable poor peasants in drought prone Marathwada, and struggle for self-respect, employment and justice among Tamil

Nadu landless labourers. Through such participation will emerge political consciousness among women.

The Chipko Movement initiated in 1972-74 is an example of the powerful impact that women's initiative can have on the power brokers, contractors and family members. Thus, the record of women's participation in political processes other than the formal has been quite creditable. Of course, while women have been visible in mass movements, group upsurges and protest struggles, their presence is not felt in structured decision-making institutional settings. Even in the structures where women's participation is substantial, they have not been given positions of powers.

IV

From the above discussions one can visualise a great difficulty with the Indian political scene is that it is impossible to generalise about the interrelationship between any single factor and political behaviour. Patterns of political behaviour from different regions show different relationships, influenced as they are by inter-related factors like the social status of women, their economic position, the cultural norms, and above all the region outlook towards women's participation in the wider society. Then again, there are some situations which are conspicuous by obvious contradictions. Kerala, which has a record of rapid growth in women's political mobilisation and women's literacy, also has a record of electing very few women members to the legislature. In contrast, Uttar Pradesh, with its general low profile of women's political participation, has persistently elected a large number of women to the legislature. On the whole, it would not be correct to state that the women's decade has forced all political parties to be alert to women's problems. The major contention of the left parties that women's problems will get solved once a classbes society is established, still continues. However, under the pressure of women members, at least the inclusion of women's issues in their manifestos has been feasible. Yet, access to significant decision-making positions in political parties continues to elude women. Today, very few women hold crucial positions.

In fact, one of the main reasons for the growth of autonomous women's groups is the disillusionment that arises, owing to a consideration of women by some political parties as peripheral elements, inspite of their involvement in day-to-day political work.

REFERENCES

1. Jean Bethke Elshtain (1981) : *Public Man, Private Women—Women in Social and Political Thought*, Martin Robertson—Oxford, p. 299.
2. Govt. of India (1988) : *National Perspective Plan for Women 1988-2000 A.D.* Min. of HRD, Deptt. of Women and Child Development, p. 153.
3. *Ibid.*, p. 154.
4. *Ibid.*, p. 154.
5. *Ibid.*, p. 155.
6. Special Correspondent (1989) : 'Women Found the Going Tough', *Hindu*, Dec. 7, 1989, p. 6.

9. WOMEN'S PARTICIPATION AT THE GRASS ROOT LEVEL

Ashok Kumar

WOMEN contiibute largely to country's economy which is mainly agriculture based. Although distributive justice has been categorically underlined in all the development plans, the needs of women have not been adequately addressed.[1] However, a majority of women in rural areas attend to domestic work and those who are engaged in free collection of goods (vegetables, roots, fish, firewood, cattle feed, etc). and providing services (sewing, weaving, maintenance of kitchen gardens, orchards, poultry, etc.). The number of rural women in the age-group of 15-49 years engaged in domestic work is estimated at 43.8 million, and those engaged in free collection of goods and services is 26.6 million.[2] Although rural women constitute a large section of population of the country, their lives are still characterized by hardwork drudgery and without any basic amenities. They are trapped in the vicious circle of low income, ill-health, low nutrition, low productivity and low wages. As a result women were considered as target groups in the Community Development Programme (1952).

As far as political participation, of women are concerned, they won the right to vote as early as 1921 and have held high political offices, yet their participation in the elections has been disappointingly low. For instance, in 1984 election there were only 161 women among the 5493 candidates and Lok Sabha had only 42 members of the fair sex in a House of 545.[3] However, their turnout at the polling booths have increased from 38.8 per cent in 1957 polls to 58 per cent in 1984 elections. The need of the hour, therefore, is to choose more women candidates and encourage them to actively take part in politics too.

During the Second, Third, Fourth and Fifth Five Year Plans programme for and participation of women did not receive any fresh impetus and continued on the earlier lines. But Rural Development programmes for women have only in recent decades recognised the crucial role of organisation and mobilisation as strategies for women's improvement and development. The programme envisaged under community development had a strong component for women's development, social education, etc. But the emphasis was more on women's role in household activities rather than community participation.

Recognising the importance of democratic institution at grass root level, the Panchayat (village council) at village level was established in 1961.[4] The Panchayati Raj institutions were in fact, considered to be the most effective instruments for realising the goals of economic betterment and social justice for the least privileged. Participation of women, who constitute nearly half of the population, in Panchayati Raj institution has been considered essential for enabling them to participate effectively and independently in democratic and political processes and to influence decision-making. It has been recognised as a step towards equal society and a means of realising the development goals for women.

In the light of this introductory statement, the aim of this paper is to examine women's participation in grass-roots level organisations. An attempt has also been made to document the main conditioning factors influencing women's participation in different developmental programmes.

II

Participation is generally understood as a process and not as some kind of static and product of development. The concept of time in terms of a process of participation is, of course, related to the task to be undertaken, which itself is a function of the development perspective employed.[5] However, participation of women in the Panchayats has been considered essential for enabling them to participate effectively in democratic processes.

The introduction of 'Democratic Decentralisations' resulted in the establishment of Panchayat. But in most of the Panchayat Raj legislations enacted by different State Governments, women were to be coopted under special category.[6] This did not result into the development of village leadership among women and their participation in the decision-making process. In this connection the Committee on the Status of Women in the Panchayati Raj Institutions has not been effective either in articulating women's needs, or in mobilising women for adequate participation. Taking note of this fact the Committee on Panchayati Raj Institutions recommended (a) increasing representation of women in these institutions ; (b) establishing a special committee of women panchayat members and powers and funds to ensure that the decisions are made by women themselves on priorities and choice in welfare and development programmes specifically for women and children ; (c) provision of institutional finance and budget support for rural industrialisation projects for women, and (d) strengthening the construtive decision-making and managerial roles ; (e) Mahila Mandals to ensure full access to development resources and services.[7]

The World Conference on Agrarian Reforms and Rural Development (WCARRD) had also recommended that Governments should "promote collective action and organisation by rural women to facilitate their participation in the full range of public services and to enhance their opportunities to participate in economic, political and social activities on an equal footing with men".

It is thus, evident that local bodies at village level are required to play a meaningful role in promoting women's participation in development. Hence, it is increasingly felt that after four decades' experience what the performance of this institution is. For this purpose, state-wise data on number of Panchayati Raj Bodies (1979-80) are presented in Table 9.1.

TABLE 9.1

State-wise Number of Panchayati Raj Bodies (1979-80)

Sl. No.	State/Union Territory	Gram Panchayat (Nos.)	Panchayat Samitis (Nos.)	Zilla Parishad (Nos.)
1	2	3	4	5
1.	Andhra Pradesh	16,137	324	21
2.	Assam	714	—	20
8.	Bihar	11,378	578	8
4.	Gujarat	12,924	182	19
5.	Haryana	5,260	87	—
6.	Himachal Pradesh	2,355	69	1
7.	Jammu & Kashmir	1,482	—	—
8.	Karnataka	8,184	175	19
9.	Kerala	1,001	—	—
10.	Madhya Pradesh	16,233	459	—
11.	Maharashtra*	24,016	296	25
12.	Manipur	107	6	—
13.	Meghalaya	—	—	—
14.	Nagaland	—	—	—
15.	Orissa	3,832	314	—
16.	Punjab	10,610	118	12
17.	Rajasthan	7,292	236	2[illegible]
18.	Sikkim	215	—	—

1	2	3	4	5
19.	Tamil Nadu	12,582	376	24
20.	Tripura	689	—	—
21.	Uttar Pradesh	72,826	876	56
22.	West Bengal	3,242	324	15
23.	Arunachal Pradesh	701	48	5
24.	A&N Islands	38	—	—
25.	Chandigarh*	21	1	1
26.	D&N Haveli	10	1	—
27.	Delhi	204	—	—
28.	Lakshadweep	—	—	—
29.	Goa, Daman & Diu	195	—	—
30.	Mizoram	—	—	—
31.	Pondicherry	—	11	—
	Total (All-India)	2,12,248	4,481	251

*Information relates to 1978-79.
Sources : Rural Development Statistics, NIRD, Hyderabad, 1982.

It is evident from Table 9.1 that Uttar Pradesh being the largest state in terms of population has the maximum number of Gram Panchayats (72,826), Panchayat Samitis (876) and Zilla Parishads (56), followed by Maharashtra and Madhya Pradesh. Contrary to this, there are some States and Union Territories viz. Meghalava, Nagaland and Lakshadweep, Mizoram, which do not have any Gram Panchayat at all.

As per 1980s counts, on an average, number of population and village in India come to 2,098 and 2.8 respectively. These two averages were maximum in Kerala because of the densely populated state. And average number of Gram Panchayats per Panchayat Samiti and Panchayat Samitis per Zilla Parishad in India were 47.4 and 17.8 respectively (Table 9.2).

The data regarding women's participation in Panchayati Raj Bodies (1979-80) for all India, are presented in Table 9.3. However, the extent of Women's participation in Panchayati Raj Bodies is derived from Table 9.2 and Table 9.3 and presented in Table 9.4.

TABLE 9.2

State-wise Coverage of Panchayati Raj Institutions

Sl. No.	State/Union Territory	Average population/ Gram Panchayat	Average No. of Village Gram Panchayat	Average No. of Gram Panchayat/ Panchayat Samities	Average No. of Pancha-yat Samiti/ Zilla Parishad
1	2	3	4	5	6
1.	Andhra Pradesh	2,281	1.8	49.8	15.4
2.	Assam	18,007	29.1	—	—
3.	Bihar	4,458	6.9	19.8	18.6
4.	Gujarat	1,512	1.4	71.0	9.6
5.	Haryana	1,517	1.3	60.5	—
6.	Himachal Pradesh	1,367	7.2	34.1	5.8
7.	Jammu & Kashmir	2,604	4.7	—	—
8.	Karnataka	2,710	3.6	46.8	9.2
9.	Kerala	18,781	1.2	—	—
10.	Madhya Pradesh	2,132	4.7	35.4	—
11.	Maharashtra	1,445	1.6	81.1	11.8
12.	Manipur	5,607	4.8	17.8	—
13.	Orissa	5,245	13.5	12.2	—
14.	Punjab	1,254	1.2	89.9	9.9
15.	Rajasthan	2,910	4.9	30.9	9.1
16.	Sikkim	847	1.9	—	—
17.	Tamil Nadu	2,551	1.3	33.5	15.7
18.	Tripura	2,444	1.3	—	—
19.	Uttar Pradesh	1,043	1.6	83.1	15.6
20.	West Bengal	10,138	11.7	10.0	21.6
21.	A&N Islands	1,763	4.5	—	—
22.	Arunachal Pradesh	583	4.0	14.6	9.6
23.	Chandigarh	2,238	1.0	21.0	1.0
24.	D&N Haveli	7,400	7.2	10.0	—
25.	Delhi	2,941	1.3	—	—
26.	Goa, Daman & Diu	3,287	2.3	—	—
27.	Pondicherry	—	—	—	—
	All India	2,098	2.8	47.4	17.8

Note : There is no Panchayati Raj set-up in Meghalaya, Nagaland, Lakshadweep and Mizoram.

Source : Same as for Table 9.1.

TABLE 9.3

Women's Participation in Panchayati Raj Bodies 1979-80--All India

Sl. No.	Item	Number
1.	Women Members of Gram Panchayats	
	(a) Elected	41,207
	(b) Coopted	1,00,385
	(c) Total	1,41,592
2.	Women Members of Panchayat Samitis	
	(a) Elected	595
	(b) Coopted	1,136
	(c) Total	1,731
3.	No. of Women Sarpanches	506

Source : Same as for Table 9.1.

TABLE 9.4

Extent of Women's Participation in Panchayati Raj Bodies

Sl. No.	Item	Percentage
1.	Percentage of elected women members of Gram Panchayat	19.41 (29.10)*
2.	Percentage of coopted women members of Gram Panchayat to Total number of Gram Panchayats	47.29 (70.90)*
3.	Percentage of elected women members of Panchayat Samitis to total number of Panchayat Samitis	13.27
4.	Percentage of coopted women members of Panchayat Samitis to total number of Panchayat Samitis	25.35
5.	Percentage of women Sarpanches to total number of Gram Panchayats	0.23

Note : Percentage of total, elected plus coopted.

The above Table 9.4 reveals that the participation of women in Panchayati Raj Institutions were very marginal. Out of 2,12,248 Gram Panchayats only 506 (0.23 per cent) women sarpanches were elected. The number of elected women members were very few (29.10 per cent) as compared to those of coopted (70.90 per cent) in both the cases, Gram Panchayats as well as Panchayat Samitis. Further, if we have a look at the elected women members of Gram Panchayat to total number of Panchayats, it was only about one-fifth (19.41 per cent). Again, in the Panchayat Samitis, a little more than one-fourth (25.35 per cent), women members were coopted and only 13.27 per cent were elected.

However, the above statistics exhibit that women's participation in the Panchayati Raj is not upto the mark. It is felt that mere reservation will not solve the problem unless women members are given commensurate powers to function effectively. Panchayats should be given real autonomy and not subjected to excessive governmental controls. And then only women members of Panchayats will welcome the concepts of Nayaya Panchayats.

Leadership, Role of Women

Women are considered an extremely pivotal point in the process of change in rural areas. The establishment of the Institution of Village Council (Panchayat) at village level in 1961 also provided opportunities to women to participate in the decision-making process. Women's participation in these bodies was encouraged by coopting them as a special category.[8] Women's participation in village-based institutions proved to be the most effective instrument in bringing about a change in their way of life in terms of economic well being and adoption of new technology.[9] Although these measures have not yielded the results to the desired extent, it cannot be denied that rural women have been exposed to the process of modernisation and avenues for interaction with the forces of social change.

While organising women's groups, an attempt was made on a country-wide basis to utilise these institutions to promote people's participation and as catalyst to social change. As these organisations were formed on democratic principles, the rural women tended to get community welfare affairs and participate in the development process by assuming leadership roles. Although the emerging village leadership, as has been found by a number of scholars,[10] is confined to the upper castes/classes in village communities, the poor women also get the opportunity, and assume leadership roles, though to a limited extent, and get exposed to the process of modernisation and social change.

Participation of women in the village based on formal and non-formal organisations has thus, made significant changes in their social status as well as their position within the family. Further, mere participation of women in these organisations is a clear indication of a change in the traditional norms which restricted free movements of a female member in society for social and political activities ; women were expected to participate in such economic and social activities which were confined to the domestic spheres. Any deviation from this norm naturally resulted in an improvement in her position in the society. Participation of women in different organisations thus have two important connotations (i) it gives them a status in the society, and (ii) it permits contribution of women not only in rural development process but also for their own development. It also gives them an opportunity to (a) work in groups on project of common interest, (b) associate with the on-going development programmes ; (c) participate in the decision-making process (d) articulate women's needs, (e) leadership in the national development process.[11]

The emerging women leadership in rural areas is to a large extent characterised by middle age, high literacy rate and income. However, in the light of the socio-economic features of the village leadership, it will be found that the characteristic features of women leadership in rural India are at variance in terms of age, education and occupation. As a result, the rural women have, in the first instance, been able to identify themselves as an important segment in the society. It has also helped in attracting the attention of the official functionaries to design and implement programmes for the benefit of women.

This is evident from the fact that a number of specific programmes specifically meant for women beneficiaries in the field of education, health, employment, family welfare, vocational training have been designed and implemented in recent years.

As a result, rural women have also started showing considerable interest in organizing joint economic ventures such as thrift societies dairy cooperatives, poultry and cattle farming, agricultural and allied activities, weaving and so on. The nature of these groups vary from place to place depending upon their pattern of work and availability of technical and financial assistance from outside. The change from home based action which has prevailed all along to collective action has made a significant change in the life style of people.

However, the introduction of women's organizations and the consequent emergence of women leadership at the grass-roots level has brought about social changes in the rural women's life, in particular and village communities in general. These organisations have the necessary potential for bringing about more changes rapidly and if given proper opportunity and assistance these can provide further strides in the development of rural women.

Economic Motivation of Women

Development programmes for women should be addressed to the problems that concern rural women [12] Economic motivation is central to rural women's behaviour. Women need money not only to contribute to the family as a whole but also to save for emergencies when they and their families are in distress.[13] Thus, when a women is urgently concerned with her family's economic and social security, she may not be interested in acquiring modern knowledge in nutrition or health practices or in literacy classes which, though related to her primary needs, are of secondary importance to her. However, once a certain amount of economic security has been achieved, rural women will be interested in other social changes desired for comprehensive development of the community and society. If national policy favours keeping rural women in economically productive work, then training and employment of rural women would be required for their effective participation.

The National Perspective Plan (1988-2000 A.D.) suggested the need for proper training for all women members of Panchayats and other bodies to enable them to exercise their authority adequately. A massive conscientization programme for women in general needs to be taken up and modules designed for this purpose should adequately deal with social economic constraints which restrict their participation in political processes and institutional structure of democracy. Separate allocations are required to be made for this purpose. There is need to link women's development programmes with Panchayat and local functionaries for effective participation of women in development.

Popular Participation

Popular participation has been conceptualised in relation to some form of political democracy and, of societal change and growth that term "development" suggests.[14] More commonly in development literature it is examined from the point of view of government intervention in development, and in this respect, terms such as "mobilisation" and "coercion" have been used to characterise the nature of the "participation", conversely, where "participation" emerges as a result of some kind of bottom-up process, it is characterised as being "authentic" and focusing on distribution.

Recently, a National Conference was held at New Delhi to discuss the issue of women's participation in Panchayati Raj bodies. It is, however, felt that mere reservation will not solve the problem unless women members are given commensurate powers to function effectively. The need to link women's development programmes with Panchayat and local functionaries for effective participation of women in development was also highlighted. The formal reservation of women in Panchayati Raj structures through reservation of seats, election, etc. is not a sufficient condition for their effective participation unless and until it is supplemented by measures which help in resolving the socio-economic pressures inhibiting them. The same can be realised by mobilising women through awareness campaigns and inter-personal communication by implementing the scheme which help them in attaining economic independence and by enhancing educational facilities at their doorsteps.

III

To summarise up, the condition of women crucially depends on the extent of economic independence and it has been observed that Indian women are lagging behind in this sphere. The long term trend in economic participation of women indicates an overall decline in percentage of workers to total female population. Here, there is one aspect which need to be considered from a policy point of view, that there is a need to replace the traditional value system, which is based on an inequality of sexes where the females play a subordinate role, with a more egalitarian system. Even if there is no absolute equality between the sexes, there is need to bring about a betterment in the quality of life for women.

Recently, over twenty-seven schemes have been initiated by the Government for the welfare of women. The strategy is to tackle the issue on three main fronts—education, employment and health. It is observed that in most of the programmes women as a group have been neglected. Hence, it is suggested that Panchayati Raj institutions can act as a link between the service agencies at the higher levels and women's group.

It will be wrong to think that Panchayati Raj should be viewed as a God that has failed. It has many achievements to its credit, the more important of which may be identified here. Politically its inception hasbecome democratic seed-drilling in the Indian soil, making an average citizen more conscious of his rights than before. Administratively, it bridged the gulf between the bureaucratic elite and the people. Socially, it generated a new leadership which was young having a modern and pre-social outlook. Finally, viewed from the developmental angle, it helped rural people to cultivate a developmental psyche.

As far as women's participation in the Panchayati Raj is concerned, it is not up to the mark. It is observed that mere reservation will not solve the problem unless women members are given commensurate powers to function effectively. However, in this regard the following steps have been suggested :

(i) all women members of panchayats and other executive bodies must be trained and empowered to exercise their authority,

(ii) particular attention must be paid to the development of inter-personal communication skills amongst the trainees/community leaders

(iii) efforts are required to elicit participation of women through establishing links between the elected representatives and the development functionaries;

(iv) programmes meant for women's development should be linked with panchayat/local functionaries for more effective participation of women.

(v) despite being members of these democratic bodies or even their head, women's political participation may be severely constrained by various socio-economic pressures. It would, therefore, be necessary to supplement formal representation in institutional structures with other measures such as mobilisation of women and involvement of panchayats on specific socio-economic issues; and

(vi) there is need to organise women workers either in a cooperative or any other form whereby production and marketing are integrated. Government institutions or voluntary welfare organisations must come forward to organise women who are self-employed and reduce their exploitation and active participation in panchayats.

REFERENCES

1. Government of India (1988) : *National Perspective Plan for Women-1988-2000 A.D.*, Report of the Core Group set-up by the Department of Women and Child Development, Ministry of Human Resource Development, Govt. of India, p. 3.

2. S.P. Jain (1985) : 'Rural Women Development in India through Last Decades', Background paper presented in an International 'Seminar on *Women and Development*, 12-16 February, p. 1.
3. *The Hindustan Times*. October, 24, 1989, New Delhi, p. 3.
4. G.K. Lieten (1988) : 'Panchayat Leaders in a West Bengal District', *Economic and Political Weekly*, Vol. XXIII, No. 40, October 1, p. 2069.
5. Peter Oakley and David Marsden (1984) : *Approaches to Participation in Rural Development*, ILO Geneva, p. 18.
6. Jain (1981) : *Op. cit.* p. 15.
7. Govt. of India (1978) : *Report of the Committee on Panchayati Raj Institutions*, Min. of Agriculture and Irrigation, Deptt. of Rural Development, New Delh.
8. S.P. Jain (1983) : 'Leadership Among Rural Women', *Social Change*, Sept. 1983, Vol. 13. No. 3, pp. 9-10.
9. V.M. Sirsikar (1970) : *The Rural Elite in a Developing Society*, Orient Longman's, New Delhi, p. 189
10. S.P. Jain and V.K. Reddy (1981) : *Rural Organisations : An Evalution*, NIRD, Hyderabad.
11. Tahrunnessa Abdullah (1981): 'Women's participation in rural development ; a Bangladesh pilot project', in ILO edited book, *Women in Rural Development—Critical Issues*, ILO, Geneva, p. 36.
12. A. Pearse and M. Stiefel (1979): *Inquiry into Participation—A Research Approach* (Geneva, UNRISD), Pearse and Stiefel discuss this understanding of participation in terms of a "process of incorporation".
13. Asoka Mehta Committe Report.
14. E.V. Prakash Rao (1987) : 'Operational Dynamics of Panchayati Raj' *Kurukshetra*, Vol. XXXV, No. 9, June, p. 15.

10. PLANNING FOR YOUNG WOMEN

H.K. Varshney

Introduction

OUR Government is committed to improve the status of women in India. The Indian Constitution provides for not only equal rights and privileges for all citizens ; but specifically mentions the need for making special provisions for women. Since the First Five Year Plan, various welfare and development schemes have been introduced to improve the living conditions of women and to increase their access to and control over material and social resources. The last assessment was made in 1975, at the beginning of the Decade for Women The facts contained in the report prepared by the Committee on the Status of Women in India (CSWI) were startling as they revealed how little had been done for women in the 28 years since Independence despite the promises and provisions contained in the Constitution. The report outlined how certain development programmes, instead of enhancing women's status, had adversely affected a large section of women and had led to, among other things, a decline in the sex ratio, a lowered life expectancy at birth, higher infant and maternal mortality, declining work participation rate among women, greater illiteracy and rising migration.

Past Attempt

These facts necessarily meant that future development plans would have to be devised to ensure that their impact on women was not ignored. The report emphasised the need to integrate women with development, to see them as 'critical input', rather than the recipients of welfare. The key shift in approach was from organising programmes that resulted in women depending on government generosity to those that would equip them with the skills and wherewithals to attain economic independence.

To implement this new thinking, a National Plan of Action was devised in 1976 and a Women's Welfare and Development Bureau was set up under the Ministry of Social Welfare.

The CSWI report, therefore, played on important role in setting up the structures to monitor programmes for women and in turn also influenced the direction of the Sixth Five Year Plan which accepted that women's lack of access to resources was an important constraint in their development. The Seventh Plan has gone a step further by first of all recognising that it is not enough to aim programmes at the family as a unit but at women specifically. Secondly, it attempts to implement the twin concerns of 'equity and empowerment'. For the first time, in the Sixth Five Year Plan, a special chapter was devoted to women which outlined various schemes to promote employment opportunities for women at different levels and to create the needed channels for women to participate effectively in decisions that affect their lives. It was also emphasized that grass-root level organisations would be promoted and Mahila Mandals and other voluntary organisations would be encouraged. However, various empirical studies have shown that women have not benefited adequately from development efforts made in the country.

The development of women, who constitute about 50 per cent of the human resources for the country have been recognised as a crucial factor in national progress and development. Various conferences and seminars have brought out the point forcefully that women's integration in all sectors of economic and social policy is necessary for national development. Therefore, in recent years there has been a growing awareness in the country of the need to involve women in development programmes in a systematic way. Social change, advancement in education along with the economic need to supplement the family income has brought forward women as a potential labour force in the economy. As such, it becomes imperative for the manpower planners to provide necessary facilities for education and skill, development to young women and also ensure ample employment opportunities for them on equal footing with men.

Education is the key that opens the door to life. Education is widely accepted as a necessary tool for attainment of development goals. Education leads to political conciousness-awareness of rights and duties among the people of a nation. In the areas of family planning, the higher the level of women education, the fewer children she is likely to have and the later she will start having them. This link between female education and lowered fertility is crucial. Some uncontrolled fertility aggravates many women's own specific health problems and also affects the health of the whole family. Therefore, it becomes the responsibility of the educational system to provide adequate facilities to women, equip them with knowledge, skills and attitudes so that they may be able to get into avenues relevant to their respective fields. In short, the quality of education is a crucial element in shaping the 'women resource' for economic development. Despite the large expansion in educational facilities from primary to university levels, women's education still lags. It may be worth mentioning here that all the draft plans and policies for uplifting the women-folk has not resulted in much progress. It is desirable that the current 'Draft National' perspective plan on development policies for women for the next 12 years i.e. A.D. 2000 deals with certain basic issues raised in that paper. It may be noted that about 75 per cent of Indian women are still illiterate. Between 1951 and 1981, the number of illiterate women had increased by 50 percent (from 162 million in 1951 to 242 million in 1981) and that for every 100 illiterates among men, the number of illiterate women had risen from 105 in 1951 to 132 in 1981. A considerable proportion of workers, especially women workers, in public and private enterprises and in government and quasi-government organisations still continue to be illiterate.

An analysis had been made in this paper regarding young women in the age-group of 15-34 years—their educational and employment pattern based on the 1981 Census and the Directorate General of Employment and Training data, in order to highlight the problems areas which needed attention of the planners. Section I deals with the composition and general characteristics of young women. Section II deals with employment situation and Section III gives the conclusion.

Human Resource Development covers the development and productive utilisation of male as well as female manpower. After more than three decades of manpower planning and development, one is compelled to admit that not much attention has been given to the development and proper utilisation of women human resources.

SECTION I

COMPOSITION AND CHARACTERISTICS

The latest population figures are available from the 5 per cent sample data of the Census of India 1981. Table 10.1 shows that out of India's total population of 665 million in 1981, youth (in the age group of 15-34 years) accounted for 214.5 million (about 32 per cent of the total population). The female population in 1981 was 321 million : 247 million females living in rural areas and 74 million females living in urban areas. The young women population in the age group of 15-34 years was 104 millions or 32.47 per cent of the total female population. Distributing the youth population in the age groups of : 15-19, 20-24, 25-29 and 30-34

TABLE 10.1

Young Women Population in India—Census-1981

(in thousand)

Age group (years)	Total Population	Women Population		
		Total	Rural	Urban
1	2	3	4	5
All ages	665,288	321,257	247,554	73,804
15—19	64,037	30,160	22,342	7,808
20—24	57,308	28,345	20,872	7,473
25—29	550,747	24,998	18,512	6,486
30—34	42,442	20.843	15,378	4,965
Youth Total	214,535	104,336	77,604	25,732

Note ; Due to rounding during estimation, totals may not tally exactly in some cases.

Source : Census of India, 1981, series-I (India), Part II, Special Report and Tables based on 5 per cent sample data.

years, it was observed that the proportion of young women was maximum in the age group of 15-19 years and decreased steadily in the following groups both in the case of rural and urban areas. In the rural areas, young women population was 77.6 million (31.35 per cent of the total rural female population whereas urban young women population was 26.7 million (36.22 per cent of the total urban female population).

Table 10.2 shows, that according to 1981 Census, the All India literacy rate was 36.25 per cent ; 26 65 per cent for rural areas and 57 4 per cent for urban areas. Literacy rate in case of females at all India, rural and urban areas were 24.82 per cent, 17.96 per cent and 47.82 per cent respectively. The wide difference between the literacy rates of total population and female population is alarming. There is still a wide gap between the educational status of males and females. Moreover, the literacy rates of females in urban areas was two to three times the literacy rates in rural areas which indicates that education is still out of reach to a very large proportion of women. The higher literacy rates in the age group of 15-19 years as compared to the higher age groups suggests that with the passage of time the literacy is also going up. Some of significant findings of 1981 census are :

(i) Indian girls dropped out of school much faster in 1981 than 1971.

(ii) Girls are being pulled out of school and put to work.

(iii) In 1981 the per cent of girls completed primary school dropped to 33 per cent from 35 per cent in 1971, but in rural areas the drop out was much sharper to 43 from 37 per cent.

This has adversely affected our women manpower resources and hence greater emphasis must now be given to this issue.

The 5 percent sample data of Census, 1981 provide valuable information on the educational and occupational characteristics of the population of literate young women. The 1981 census, has distinguished two categories of workers : Main workers and Marginal workers. The definition of Main workers and Marginal workers is given as follows :—

TABLE 10.2

Young Women Literacy Rates by Age and Strata in India—Census 1981

(Percentage)

Age Group (years)	PERSONS			WOMEN		
	T	R	U	T	R	U
1	2	3	4	5	6	7
All ages	36.23	29.65	57.80	24.82	17.96	47.82
15—19	55.37	47.74	76.86	43.28	33.66	70.40
20—24	52.02	43.11	74.71	37.18	27.16	65.16
25—34	45.10	36.25	69.50	28.96	19.64	56.98

"Main workers are those who have worked for the major part of the year preceding the date of enumeration and whose main activity was in either cultivation or as agricultural labourer or in household industry or in other work. Marginal workers are those who have not worked for the major part of the preceding year concerned but nevertheless have done some work during any time in the reference period. In other words, such workers while not being capable of being classified as main workers, nevertheless perform some work."

In the 1981 census, total work force was 244.61 million, of which 222.52 million were main workers and 22.09 million marginal workers. Thus, of the total Indian population, 36.77 per cent are in the working force and 33.45 per cent are main workers and only 3.32 per cent are marginal workers of the total main workers. 44.97 million are females which is about 14 per cent of the total female population and 20.21 per cent of the total main workers. Total female marginal workers in the Indian economy account for 18.55 millions which are 5.77 per cent of the total female population and about 84 per cent of the total marginal workers.

Table 10.3 shows that in the rural areas, more than 80 per cent of the workforce consists of main workers but in the case of females, the share of marginal workers is as large as 31 per cent. About half of the main workers belong to young age, both in the aggregate as well as for females. The relative shares of women main workers in the age-groups of 15-19, 20-24, 25-29 and 30-34 years are 26.24 per cent, 26.14 per cent, 24.96 per cent and 22.66 per cent respectively. Out of female marginal workers, 55.66 per cent belong to the young age group (15-34 years). Table 10.4 shows that in urban areas, more than 97 per cent of the workforce comprises main workers and the proportion in case of females being 87.5 per cent. Over one half of main workers, both in the aggregate and for females, belong to the young age group. It is important to note that females, account for only 11.65 per cent of the total main workers. In the case of marginal workers, more than 85 per cent are females. The maximum (29 per cent) and minimum (20 per

TABLE 10.3

Main Workers and Marginal Workers among Young Women in Rural India by Age-group - Census 1981

(in thousand)

Age Group	TOTAL WORK FORCE		WOMEN WORK FORCE	
	Main workers	Marginal workers	Main workers	Marginal workers
1	2	3	4	5
All ages	176,434	30,874	39,603	17,785
15—19	19,595	2,936	5,088	2,286
20—24	21,847	3,953	5,069	2,423
25—29	21,918	2,612	4,840	2,280
30—34	19,381	2,208	4,394	2,081
Youth Total	82,741	10,709	19,391	9,010

TABLE 10.4

Main Workers and Marginal Workers among Young Women in Urban India by Age-group—Census-1981

(in thousand)

Age Group	Total Work Force		Women Work Force	
	Main Workers	Marginal Workers	Main Workers	Marginal Workers
1	2	3	4	5
All ages	46,083	1,214	5,370	767
15—19	3,109	201	483	121
20—24	6,188	200	691	98
25—29	7,163	182	790	124
30—34	6,396	121	730	86
Youth Total	23,064	704	2,694	429

cent) employment of female marginal workers were observed in the age of 25-29 years and 30-34 years.

Occupational and educational analysis in this paper is confined to 'main workers' only. It is evident from Table 10.5 that 43.4 per cent of female main workers in urban areas are literate, while only 11.8 per cent are literate in rural areas. The proportion of literates among the principal industrial groups for both rural and urban areas are shown in this Table. It is clear from the table that both in rural and urban households, literate female main workers are being absorbed in Transport, Trade and allied activities. Given opportunities for gaining education and skills, non-household industry could also merge in the future as a significant venue for providing employment to female workers in rural and urban areas. Therefore, it becomes necessary for manpower planners to develop the skills of women for tertiary activities for proper manpower utilisation.

The special reports of the Registrar General on the basis of the 5 per cent sample provided significant information on the educational level of young women and reveals an inherent weakness in the education system of our country. Table 10.6

TABLE 10.5

Female Main Workers in India Classified by Industrial Category and Literacy—Census 1981

	Industrial Category	Female Main Workers			
		Rural		Urban	
		Number (000)	Literacy (%)	Number (000)	Literacy (%)
	1	2	3	4	5
I	Cultivators	14,682	11.7	250	20.8
II	Agricultural Labourers	19,878	7.6	890	11.1
III	Livestock, Forestry, Fishing, Hunting & Plantations Orchard & Allied Activities	733	15.0	100	27.0
IV	Mining and Quarrying	134	3.7	29	13.8
V	(a) Manufacturing, Processing, Servicing & Repair, Household industry	1,501	20,9	563	32.7
V	(b) Manufacturing. Processing, Servicing & Repair, Non-household Industry	830	30.7	768	44.7
VI	Construction	201	7.5	157	13.4
VII	Trade & Commerce	438	21.2	479	42.4
VIII	Transport, Storage and Communication	47	44.7	123	62.6
XI	Other Services	1,159	53.7	2,012	65 9
	Total	39,603	11.8	5,370	43.4

Note : Due to rounding during estimation, totals may not tally exactly in some cases.

and 10.7 gives data regarding literacy among young women for both rural and urban areas.

Table 10.6 gives the literacy rates in the various age groups of young women for rural areas. Of the total 19.4 million young women main workers, only 3.16 million (16.-8 per cent) are literate. Among them 28.7 per cent are without any formal education, 42.8 per cent educated upto primary level and 15.2 per cent are educated upto middle level. On the other hand, technical/non-technical diploma or certificate holders are only 1.5 per cent ; and 2.4 per cent are graduate and above.

The decline in the proportion of young women persuing education beyond primary level is mainly due to economic compulsions, lack of educational facilities and social constraints like early marriage. Further, rural young women who are going in for higher education largely prefer general education as compared to technical ed cation. The reason for this can be attributed as much to availability of enough employment opportunities in rural areas for non-technical services as to lack of technical training facilities in rural areas.

Table 10.7 gives literacy rates and educational levels in the various age groups of young women for urban areas. Of the total 2.7 million young women main workers, 1.5 million (54.1 per cent) are literate. Among them 9.9 per cent are without any formal education, 16.8 per cent are educated upto primary level ; 10.4 per cent middle and 23.4 per cent have obtained matriculate/secondary certificate. Though only 3.3 per cent females are technical/non-technical diploma holders, 27.7 per cent are graduate and above. Hence it can be safely deduced that after higher secondary, females are attracted towards conventional education *viz*. B.A., M.A.. etc. and not towards vocational education.

Table 10.9 gives the distribution of young women main workers in India by age-group and industrial category. Of the total 45 million female main workers, ›1 6 per cent are engaged in the primary sector ; 8.9 per cent in the secondary sector ; and 9.5 per cent in tertiary sector. Among female main workers, 22.1 million (i.e., 49 per cent) belong to the young age category between age groups of 15-34 years. Among the young

TABLE 10.6

Young Women Main Workers in Rural India by Age-Group and Literacy—Census-1981

(in thousand)

Educational Level	Age Group (years)						
	All ages	15—19	20—24	25—29	30—34	Youth Total	Col. (7) as percentage to literate youth total
1	2	3	4	5	6	7	8
Literate (without educational level)	1,561	303	242	202	158	905	28.7
Primary	1,905	453	393	302	203	1,351	42.8
Middle	616	151	154	109	65	479	15.2
Matriculation/Secondary	329	36	79	77	58	250	7.9
Hr. Secondary/Intermediate/ Pre-university	56	4	15	17	10	46	1.5
Non-Technical Dip./Cert. not equal to degree	18	—	2	4	4	10	0.3
Technical Dip./Cert. not equal to degree	76	—	7	13	19	39	1.2
Graduate and above	103	—	17	33	25	75	2.4
Total Literates	4,664	949	910	755	543	3.157	100.0

Note : Due to rounding during estimation, totals may not tally exactly in some cases.

TABLE 10.

Young Women Main Workers in Urban India by Age-Group and Literacy—Census 1981

(in thousand)

Educational Level	All ages	Age Group (years) 15—19	20—24	25—29	30—34	Total Youth	Col. (7) as percentage to literate youth total
1	2	3	4	5	6	7	8
Literate (without educational level	286	41	37	36	30	144	9.9
Primary	410	75	67	55	48	245	16.8
Middle	249	37	46	37	32	152	10.4
Matriculation/Secondary	538	27	95	113	105	340	23.4
Hr. Secondary/Intermediate/ Pre-university	171	7	39	44	32	122	8.4
Non-Technical Dip./Cert. not equal to degree	18	—	2	3	4	9	0.6
Technical Dip./Cert. not equal to degree	73	1	9	14	16	40	2.7
Graduate & above	588	4	109	169	122	404	27.8
Total Literates	2333	192	404	471	389	1456	100.00

TABLE 10.8

Distribution of youths attending/school college by age, sex and strata

(percentage)

Age Group (years)	Total			Rural			Urban		
	Persons	Males	Females	Persons	Males	Females	Persons	Males	Females
1	2	3	4	5	6	7	8	9	10
15—19	26.4	36.0	15.5	20.5	30.9	8.9	42.9	50.2	34.5
20—24	7.2	11.3	3.0	4.7	8.2	1.3	13.4	18.5	7.5
25—34	1.1	1.7	0.5	0.8	1.3	0.3	3.0	2.7	1.1

age category 80.5 per cent women main workers are engaged in the primary, 10.1 per cent in the secondary and 9.4 per cent in the tertiary sectors. The maximum concentration for both primary (84 per cent) and secondary (11.5 per cent) sector was observed in the age groups of 15-19 years whereas in the tertiary sector, the maximum concentration was observed in the age group of 30-34 years.

The work participation rates for young women main workers by various age groups and strata have been given in Table 10.10. The overall work participation rate for females was 14.0 per cent whereas for rural and urban areas the participation rates were 16.0 per cent and 7.3 per cent respectively. The work participation rates for young women in the aggregate and for rural and urban areas were 21.2 per cent, 25.0 per cent and 10.1 per cent respectively. This indicates that young women account for a higher proportion of female employment especially in rural areas. Among young women, work participation rate increases with age, both in rural and urban areas. In rural areas, it increased from 22.8 per cent in 15-19 years to 27.7 per cent in 30-34 years whereas in urban areas it increased from 6.2 per cent in 15-19 years to 14.7 per cent in 30-34 years.

This is inspite of the efforts made by the government in recent years for the vocationalisation of education, especially for the females. These tables bring out a significant fact that inspite of spread of primary and secondary education and adult education programmes development of potential female human resources still lags behind seriously. This must now be a matter of utmost concern for educational planners specially in the wake of the new educational policy.

The concept, whether a person was attending an educational institution i.e., school/college was first introduced in the 1981 census. The distribution of youths attending school/college by sex and strata has been presented in Table 10.8. Among the given age groups the largest proportion of students is in 15-19 years age-groups, which stands at 26.4 per cent. This male-female differential is higher in rural areas as compared to urban areas in all the age-groups. The proportion

TABLE 10.9

Young Women : Main workers in India by Age-group and Industrial Category

[(in thousand)

Industrial Category	Age-Group (years)					
	All ages	15—19	20—24	25—29	30—34	Youth Total
1	2	3	4	5	6	7
I	14,932	1,787	1,856	1,777	1,632	7,052
II	20,768	2,772	2,668	2,518	3,293	10.251
III	832	100	107	105	84	396
IV	163	20	22	25	24	91
Sub Total - Primary Sector	36,695 (81.6)	4,679 (84.0)	4 653 (80.6)	4,425 (78.6)	4,033 (78.7)	17,790 (80.5)
V (a)	2,064	321	289	258	222	1,090
V (b)	1,598	267	255	216	187	925
VI	358	56	55	51	43	205
Sub Total ; Secondary Sector	4,020 (8.9)	644 (11.5)	599 (10.4)	525 (9.3)	452 (8.8)	2,220 (10.1)

Table 10.9 (*Contd.*)

VII	917	46	92	100	109	366
VIII	170	12	30	34	26	102
IX	3,170	190	387	525	505	1 607
Sub Total : Tertiary Sector	4,257 (1.5)	248 (4.5)	508 (8.8)	679 (12.1)	640 (12.5)	2,075 (9.4)
Total All Industries	44,973 (100.0)	5,571 (100.0)	5,760 (100.0)	5,630 (100.0)	5,124 (100.0)	22,085 (100.0)

I : Cultivators

II : Agricultural Labourers

III : Livestock, forestry, fishing etc.

IV : Mining & quarrying.

V : Manufacturing, Processing, Servicing and Repairs
(a) Household
(b) Non-household

VI : Construction

VII : Trade & Commmerce

VIII : Transport, storage & communication.

IX : Other services.

Note : (i) Due to rounding during estimation totals may not tally exactly in some cases.
(ii) Figures in brackets represent percentage to grand total.

TABLE 10.10

Work Participation Rates for young Women Main Workers by Age and Strata : Census—1981

(Percentage)

Age Group (years)	Work Participation Rates		
	Total	Rural	Urban
1	2	3	4
All ages	14.0	16.0	7.3
15—19	18.5	22.8	6.2
20—24	20.3	24.3	9.3
25—29	22.5	26.1	12.2
30—34	24.6	27.7	14.7
Youth Total	21.2	25.0	10.0

of young women fell sharply from 15.5 per cent in the 15-19 years age-group to 3.0 per cent in 20-24 years age-group and further to 0.5 per cent in the 25-34 years age-group. The same trend was observed in rural and urban areas. The possible reasons for the low studentship of women in higher age groups may be due to :

(i) Lack of educational facilities,
(ii) Early marriage and other social constraints,
(iii) Financial constraints,

SECTION-II

EMPLOYMENT SITUATION

The information on the employment condition, future prospects for youths and their distribution according to various characteristics is available with the Directorate General of Employment and Training in the Ministry of Labour. Some relevant data which have a bearing on the policy formulation are presented in brief in Tables 10.11 to 10.14.

Table 10.11 shows the number of work-seekers registered with employment exchanges for the years 1975 to 1985 classified by sex, along with the percentage variation over the previous year. The number of work-seekers increased from 93.3 lakhs in 1975

TABLE 10.11

Number of work-seekers registered with Employment Exchanges by Sex during the years 1975-1985

Year (ending 31st December)	Number of work-seekers (,000)			Percentage change over previous year		
	Total	Men	Wofflen	Total	Men	Women
1	2	3	4	5	6	7
1975	9326.3	8201.4	1124.9	10.6	9.9	15.6
1976	9784.3	8553.6	1230.7	4.9	4.3	9.4
1977	10924.0	9513.7	1410.3	11.6	11.2	14.6
1978	12677.8	11006.2	1671.6	16.1	15.7	18.5
1979	14333.9	12429.6	1904.3	13.1	12.9	13.9
1980	16200.3	13855.1	2345.2	13.0	11.5	23.2
1981	17838.1	15105.2	2732.9	10.1	9.0	16.5
1982	19753.0	16614.6	3138.4	10.7	10.0	14.8
1983	21953 3	18371.7	3581.6	11.1	10.6	14.1
1984	23546.8	19544.7	4002.1	7.3	6.4	11.7
1985	26269.9	21322.4	4447.5	11.6	11.7	11.1

Source : Directorate General of Employment & Training (unpublished data from EMI-unit)

to 262.7 lakhs in 1985, i.e., registering an increase of 166.1 per cent during the last decade. The growth of women work-seekers was significantly higher than that of their conuter-part ; their number increased from 11.2 lakhs in 1975 to 44.5 lakhs in 1985 i.e. an increase of 295.4 per cent. This fact may be attributed to the accelerated growth in women's education and the changing value of the society where the working women is becoming a status symbol. Certain relaxations and facilities provided by the government may also be responsible in attracting educated women in the labour market.

Distribution of work-seekers by age-groups

The work-seekers are mainly concentrated in four age-groups viz. 15-19 years, 20-24 years, 25-29 years and 30-34 years and these four groups together account for about 95 per cent of the total registrants. Table 10.12 presents the distribution of young work-seekers by sex and age-groups as on the end of December 1984. The table shows that out of 195.4 lakh men and 40.0 lakh women work-seekers, the relative shares in the age-groups 15-19 years, 20-24 years, 25-29 years and 30-34 years for men were 29.8 per cent, 38.5 per cent, 26.4 per cent and 10 per cent respectively and the respective shares in the case of women were 11.4 per cent, 37.9 per cent, 24.5 per cent and 10 per cent. However, the maximum concentration of work-seekers (about 38 per cent) for both the sexes was in the age-group of 20-24 years followed by work-seekers in the age-group 25-29 years (25-26 per cent.) This table further depicts that while the relative share of women work-seekers (all ages) to total work-seekers (all ages) was 17 per cent, their relative share to the total registrants in various age-groups varies between 16 per cent to 18 per cent. Thus the women work-seekers are distributed over various age groups in the same pattern as the male work-seekers.

Educated work-seekers

The work-seekers in the employment exchanges are registered without any regard to their educational qualifications. Thus illiterates, less educated as well as educated persons are on

TABLE 10.12

Distribution of work-seekers by sex and age-group

Age-group (years)	No. of work-seekers as on 31st December, 1984 (,000)			Percentage to total		
	Total	Men	Women	Total	Men	Women
1	2	3	4	5	6	7
15—19	4722.0 (100.0)	3866.8 (81.9)	855.2 (18.1)	20.1	19.8	21.4
20—24	9039.8 (100.0)	7522.0 (83.2)	1517.8 (16.3)	38.4	38.5	37.9
25—29	6134.1 (100.0)	5154.3 (84.0)	979.8 (16.0)	26.0	26.4	24.5
30—34	2357.6 (100.0)	1958.3 (83.1)	399.3 (16.9)	10.0	10.0	10.0
Total (All ages)	23546.8 (100.0)	19544.7 (83.0)	4002.1 (17.0)	100.0	10.0	100.0

Note : Figures in the brackets are percentages to the total of the respective age-groups.
Source : Directorate General of Employment & Training (unpublished data from EMI-unit).

the live register of the employment exchanges. Since the educated people are generally, interested in white collar jobs, theproblem of unemployment in the case of educated persons needs greater attention.

The distribution of work-seekers by educational level, sex and age-group has been provided in Table 10.13 and 10.14. It may be observed from these tables that out of 195.4 lakh men and 40.0 lakh women work-seekers, the proportion of educated work-seekers for males and females was only 51 per cent and 63 per cent respectively. Thus about half of the registrants were either illiterate or had qualifications below matric level. Again, of the total 125.4 lakh educated (matric and above) registrants, 100.1 lakh were men and 25.3 lakh were women. It may be noted that among the educated work-seekers, both in case of men and women, about 60 per cent were matriculates/higher secondary and about 40 per cent were graduate and above.

While analysing the data in respect of educated work-seekers (matric & above) by sex, it may be observed that the proportion of educated young women is higher as compared to men in all the educational levels. It is a pity that the Indian economy is not able to absorb the educated women and they have to wait for long period to get gainful employment. If this trend continues it will hamper the urge for education and the educational standards of women in the country will not improve. The women will continue to lag behind. It is, therefore, very necessary that special attention is given to see that all the educated women get employment within reasonable time. There should also be part time employment opportunities for child-bearing and rearing women.

SECTION-III
CONCLUSIONS

It is apparent from the present analysis that inspite of the development that has taken place, the economy still lacks the capacity to absorb annual additions to the labour force. Young women largely find employment in unorganised sector. The emphasis on educational development of young women as

TABLE 10.13

Distribution of women work-seekers by Educational Level and Age-group (at the end of Dec. 1984)

(in thousand)

Educational Level	Age group (years)									
	15—19		20—24		25—29		30—34		Total	
1	2	3	4	5	6	7	8	9	10	11
Below Matric	1710.9	271.7	3512.8	520.5	2604.1	394.0	1085.4	175.9	9533.9	1477.0
Matric	1430.8	400.5	2286.9	572.3	1355.5	303.6	489.7	123.9	5825.4	1475.8
Under Graduate (including Intermediate/Hr. Sec.)	560.2	129.7	1031.1	223.1	630.1	121.7	207.1	40.6	2526.2	549.3
Graduate	159.5	51.8	639.3	178.8	503.4	136.0	156.7	48.2	1503.7	435.6
Post Graduate	5.4	1.5	61.9	28.4	61.0	24.5	19.4	10.7	155.5	64.4
Total	3866.8	855.2	7522.0	1517.8	5154.3	979.8	1958.3	399.3	19544.7	4002.1

Sources : Directorate General of Employment & Training (unpublished data from EMI unit)

TABLE 10.14

Percentage Distribution of Work-seekers by Educational Level and Age-groups (at the end of Dec. 1984)

Educational Level	Age group (years)									
	15—19		20—24		25—29		30—34		Total (all ages)	
1	2	3	4	5	6	7	8	9	10	11
Below Matric	44.3	31.8	46.7	34.3	50.5	40.2	55.4	44.0	48.8	36.9
	(17.0)	(18.4)	(36.8)	(35.2)	(27.3)	(26.7)	(11.4)	(11.9)	(100.0)	(100.0)
Matric	37.0	46.8	30.4	37.7	26.3	31.0	25.0	31.0	29.8	36.9
	(24.6)	(27.1)	(39.3)	(38.8)	(23.3)	(20.6)	(8.4)	(8.4)	(100.0)	(100.0)
Undergraduate (including Intermediate/ Hr. Secondary)	14.5	15.2	13.6	14.7	12.2	12.4	10.6	10.2	12.9	13.7
	(22.2)	(23.6)	(40.4)	(40.6)	(24.9)	(22.2)	(8.2)	(7.4)	(100.0)	(100.0)
Graduate	4.1	6.0	8.5	11.8	9.8	13.9	8.0	12.1	7.7	10.9
	(10.6)	(11.9)	(42.5)	(41.1)	(33.5)	(31.2)	(10.4)	(11.1)	(100.0)	(100.0)
Post-graduate	0.1	0.2	0.8	1.5	1.2	2.5	1.0	2.7	0.8	1.6
	(3.5)	(2.3)	(39.8)	(36.3)	(39.2)	(38.0)	(12.5)	(16.6)	(100.0)	(100.0)
Total	100.0	100.0	100.0	100.0	100.0	100.0	100.0	100.0	100.0	100.0
	(19.8)	(21.4)	(38.5)	(37.9)	(26.4)	(24.5)	(10.0)	(100.0)	(100.0)	(100.0)

Source : Directorate General of Employment & Training (unpublished data from EMI unit)

envisaged in various plans on the one hand, and the inability of the economy to create adequate employment opportunities for them, on the other hand, is likely to further widen the mismatch between education and employment.

The salient points that emerged from the analysis are :—

— The young women are about 32.5 per cent of the total female population. Their distribution in rural and urban areas is three-fourth and one-fourth. (Table 10.1)
— literacy rate among the young women in urban area is 2 to 3 times higher than that in the rural area, (Table 10.2)
— among the total young women workers in rural areas, about 68 per cent are main workers, whereas in urban areas, the proportion is as high as 86 per cent (Table 10.3 & 10.4).
— literacy among young women "main workers" is 16.28 per cent in rural areas as compared to 54.1 per cent in urban areas (Table 10.6 & 10.7).
— Work participation rates for young women on the criterion of "main workers" in rural and urban areas are 25 per cent and 10 per cent respectively. (Table 10.10).
— the number of young women work-seekers on the live-register recorded an increase of 295.4 per cent during 1975-85 whereas in the case of men, the increase was only of the order of 166.1 per cent.
— the proportion of educated young women work-seekers is in general higher as compared to the men at all educational levels.

Thus, it can be safely concluded, that there is need to pay an attention to the problem of education and employment for women—both in rural and urban areas. Literacy rates and educational levels among young women are far from satisfactory. The fulfilment of the constitutional directive to provide free and compulsory education up to the age of 14 years continues to remain a distant dream as far as women are concerned. No wonder the high illiteracy ratio (75 per cent) among women still worries the planners. At present women are largely employed in the unorganised sector which lures them at comparatively low wage and poor facilities. The employment pattern as envisaged in our economy is a reflection of the type of training facilities available for women in India.

In India, even after 40 years of planned development, manpower imbalances in certain categories (specially among young women) do persist although these are not desirable from the point of view of either the individual or the society or the nation. In order to remove these imbalances are adjustment of manpower resources available in the country at different levels is very necessary. Manpower planning *viz-a-viz* educational planning can to a great extent help in reducing these mbalances.

11. ROLE OF VOLUNTARY ORGANISATIONS IN WOMEN'S DEVELOPMENT

Ashok Kumar & C.P. Roy

INDIA has made rapid strides in a number of fields including science and technology. But, it has also been experiencing travails of transition which a developing country is bound to face. However, for over several decades, transformation of the rural communities has been the concern of the government, the voluntary organisations, and the people. An active role in the field of child development, largely in the inaccessible parts of the country, was played by the religious missionaries since the middle of the 19th century, who aimed at an all-round development of their followers.

However, successive plan documents, reports of the commissions and committees,[1] apart from delineating the role of voluntary organisations in the field of child development in context of their terms of reference, have analysed the positive dimensions of the functioning of these organisations. The concern of the state in seeking the cooperation of these people's institutions is expressed in the plan documents. The Mid-Term Plan (1978-83) states, "the voluntary agencies who are engaged in social and developmental work are close to the people and have the capacity to motivate the rural population for community participation in developmental programmes. With a view to utilising this potential, it is contemplated that as a policy, voluntary organisations doing social and developmental work in child development areas should be induced into integrated development approach so as to provide a foil to the completely departmental approach to the problem.[2] However, in the present exercise, in broad terms, an attempt has been made to examine the role of some national level voluntary organisations in the field of child welfare activities.

The Indian women suffer from ignorance, poverty and continuing discrimination. During the last few years a number of laws pertaining to women have passed. But unfortunately the law enforcement agency is neither so strong and effective, so as to fight out against the vested interests nor is it imaginative enough to take cognizance of all the intricacies involved in the implementation of such legislation. However, for tackling these problems, the voluntary organisations have very important role to play like (i) in creating awareness among women ; (ii) in providing economic and social security ; (iii) in providing shelter to women, and (iv) Councelling, guidance and legal assistance etc.

Voluntary Organisations—its concept

According to Lord Beveridge, voluntary organisation[3] is 'one which, whether its workers are paid or unpaid, is initiated and governed by its own members without external control'. Such organisations, however, are only ideal forms. In practice, some mode of control exists either by the state or by the funding agency or by both. In some cases enlightened public opinion also acts as a check on its functioning.

Some scholars have drawn distinction between non-official organisations and voluntary organisations. To them, all non-official organisations are not necessarily voluntary. The test for voluntariness is that the organisations has to try and stimulate voluntary action in the served community. It has also to progressively incorporate enlightened individuals belonging to the community to serve in the higher echelons of its decision-making machinery. Another distinguishing point made out between these bodies is that the voluntary organisations are spontaneous in their origin whereas the non-official agencies may be sponsored by the state.

A voluntary agency has the following main features[4] :

(i) It should be voluntary and created by the people themselves at the grass-root level;

(ii) It should have a legal status through registration under an appropriate Act ;

(iii) It should have a Managing Committee elected/nominated by members ;

(iv) It should have considerable autonomy and flexibility in planning and management of its programmes and services ;

(v) It should have a sense of commitment to human development/welfare ;

(vi) It should understand people's needs and help to solve their socio-economic problems ;

(vii) It should plan and implement its own programmes through its own voluntary and paid workers ;

(viii) It should raise its funds from the community ; and

(xi) It should maintain its accounts and be accountable to people and the Governments so far as it receives grants.

Voluntary Organisation—Retrospect

As voluntary organisations had necessary flexibility, adaptability and voluntarism in them, they came forward to organise child welfare programmes much before the government initiated these programmes through its five-year plans. These voluntary organisations have been serving children in the area of health, education, nutrition, welfare and recreation.[5] They have provided both institutional and non-institutional services.

Balkanji Bari was the first children's organisation formed in the year 1920 with its headquarters in Bombay. It started nursery schools, children's club, play grounds, children's literacy programmes, child's arts and crafts. In 1924, the Guild of service launched its child welfare service in Madras and South India. In 1927, the Children's Aid Society, Bombay, established residential institutions for vagrant children. In the year 1942, Kishore Dal in Bihar was founded, Nanhi Duniya was set-up in 1946 and Bachhon Ki Biradari was formed in Delhi in 1949.[6] These organisations organised Shishu Bhavan, Children art exhibition, play centres and distributed milk to children.

During First Five Year Plan, child health, nutrition education and family planning were the main programmes undertaken by voluntary organisations. With the establishment of Central Social Welfare Board, voluntary effort in child welfare programmes got fillip. The Second Five Year Plan emphasized that voluntary effort in the field of social welfare have to be supplemented by the Central, State and Local authorities.

The Central Social Welfare Board while phasing out the community development projects consequent on the introduction of the Panchayati Raj system handed over balwadis in around 1500 villages to the voluntary organisations and the local Mahila Mandals in 1961-62 onwards. As part of the grants-in-aids of the Central Social Welfare Board, around 5,000 balwadis and equal number of creches are being run by voluntary agencies with assistance of the Board. Some important national level voluntary organisations in the field of child welfare are summarised here :

(i)	Indian Council for Child Welfare (ICCW)	: Established in 1952 under Societies Registration Act 1860. Its prime aim was to mobilise voluntary activity in every state in favour of all aspects of children's need.

(ii) Balkanji Bari : National level organisation established in 1920. Supplementing home and school activities to children.

(iii) The Children's Aid Society : The society was founded in 1927 at Bombay. Rehabilitation of destitute children was the main objective.

(iv) Harijan Sevak Sangh : Set-up in 1932 in New Delhi with aim to educate Hindus on the need of removal of untouchability. Since 1971 it runs Balwadis and creches.

(v) SOS Children's : It provides non-institutionalised form of child care. It has provision for cottage type residential care with mixed groups and provides near family atmosphere.

Some other important voluntary organisations working in the field of child welfare are the Bhartiya Adimjati Sevak Sangh, Indian Red Cross Society, the All India Women's Conference, Bhartiya Grameen Mahila Sangh, Kasturba Gandhi National Memorial Trust, the Royal Common Wealth Society for the Blind (Bombay). Children's Book Trust (New Delhi), Child Welfare Workers Association (Bombay,) Children's Film Society (Bombay). Society for the Care, Treatment and Training of Children in Need of Special Care (Bombay), and Society for the Rehabilitation of Crippled Children (Bombay).

Since last decades several innovative projects have been undertaken in voluntary sector in different parts of the country to meet the needs of children.

Some of these projects are as follows :

(i) Indo-Dutch Project for Child Welfare : At the Chevilla Block of Range Reddy district aims at overall

Experiment in an Integrated Approach.		development of children, a joint venture of the Netherlands Foundations. Govt. of India and State Govt. Started in 1969.
(ii) Integrated Mother and Child Health Nutrition Project.	:	Started in 1974 to deliver integrated health and nutrition services to on going children and mothers programmes.
(iii) Comprehensive Rural Health Project, Jamkhed.	:	Project initiated in 1970 is located in Jamkhed village in Ahmed Nagar district. To meet the basic health needs of the population by providing parental care, immunisation of children and mothers.
(iv) Integrated Health Services Project, Miraj.	:	It was designed to provide medical and health care in an integrated pattern for a vast rural population. A joint project of the Govt. of Maharashtra, Sangeli Zilla Parishad and Miraj Medical Centre.
(v) Vikasvadi Project Kosbad.	:	A simple pattern for pre-school care in rural areas. It aims at providing these services through a trained village women in basic principle of early child care including nutrition, immunisation and play techniques using ordinary local equipment. These services are provided to village children between the ages of three and six.
(vi) Project Poshak	:	A micro pilot project on integrated health nutrition for pre-school children in rural and tribal areas of Madhya Pradesh. Based on principle of take home

food for children upto three years and pregnant and lactating mothers with supportive services of child care, education and health. The project was administered by CARE India. Financial assistance was provided by USAID and the UNICEF.

(vii) Other Innovative Projects. : Cooperative Rural Dispensaries Services, Kerala, which functions as a self contained medical unit rendering day to day medical care both curative and preventive is yet another innovative project in the voluntary sector which provides medical services to people. Other projects include Padha Hospital Community Health Project in Betul district of Madhya Pradesh, Community Health Development Project, Kanyakumari, Child in Need Institute in Daulatpur village, South of Calcutta, Nutrition Rehabilitation Centre and village child care centres, Madurai, etc.

However, apart from providing services to the needy, voluntary organisations have also done commendable work in the field of training. In this context, the name of Kasturba Gandhi National Memorial Trust needs to be mentioned. The trust trained Gram Sevikas, Mukhya Sevikas and Mid-wives. Thus, voluntary organisations have been responsible for the organisation of many child welfare programmes. The Government has enhanced its support to them by providing necessary funds. Their role have not only been to promote participation of the community in the provision of services but also increase awareness of the community in regard to child care education.

The Changing Role of Voluntary Organisation

There are huge number of spiritual inspired organisations which have done commendable job particularly in the areas of health and education with a degree of dedication and devotion which other cannot hope to attain. Most of the organisations are concentrated due to a variety of historical reasons, in the Southern and Western parts of the country.

The Sarvodaya Movement, under the inspiring leadership of the late Vinoba Bhave, was able to attract a good number of leaders like Jayaprakash Narayan. The objective of Sarvodaya is to instil faith in man and his future. To reduce tension and coersion in society, sharing together of good things that are produced by common endeavours are indispensable.[8] Sarvodaya aims at replacing the present 'competitive' economy by a social economy based on cooperation.[9]

Voluntary organisations are capable of performing a wide-variety of tasks. The aims, motivations, ideology, dedication, quality of work personnel etc. differ from one agency to another. All the agencies are involved in development work in one way or the other, but they exhibit marked differences in the context, direction and quality of this involvement. Some voluntary agencies may not take up development programmes, but serve the people indirectly by placing checks on corruption and inefficiency that are usually associated with development administration.

However, the voluntarism of the post-independence India yielded place to a new kind of professional voluntarism distinct from professional politics. As a result, a new class of professionals has entered the field of voluntarism-economists, sociologists, engineers, agronomists, veterinarians, communicators, architects, managers and the rest. This professionalism of voluntarism marks a new departure. These people are committed to development, socio-economic transformation and social justice. Voluntarism has drawn talented professionals and angry young men seeking social revolution through social action. These are the militant professionals of voluntarism, social dynamics of considerable potential.[10] Social mobility and change brought about by social movements lead to soc al transformation thereby changing the traditional balance of power.[11] The increasing role of voluntary agencies in the local level planning can be attributed to.[12]

— the need to help a specific target group, e.g., women, children and the landless ;
— imparting certain skills through training to augment the income of the target groups, e.g., handicrafts, new varieties of seeds or crops ;
— to popularise social activities aimed at improving the quality of life for the disadvantaged groups, e.g. adult literacy, nutrition. education, basic health and sanitation and family planning ; and
— to popularise appropriate technologies by improving indigenous machines, tools, artifacts and demonstrating their superiority.

Depending on the approaches they adopt and the priority they give, voluntary agencies have been classified into seven categories by J.B. Singh.[13] This means that generally voluntary agencies operate in seven distinct areas. These are :

(i) Charity : Giving food, clothing, medicine, sums in cash and kind, land, buildings etc.

(ii) Welfare : Providing facilities for education, health, drinking water, roads, communication, etc.

(iii) Relief : Responding to call of duties during natural calamities like floods, drought, earthquakes and man-made calamities like refugee influx, ravages of war, etc.

(iv) Rehabilitation : Continuing and follow-up of the work in areas struck by calamities and starting activities durable in nature.

(v) Services : Building up infrastructure in depressed backward areas. Tractor

	hiring services, providing or facilitating credit, supply of seeds, fertilisers, technical know-how, etc.
(vi) Development of socio-economic environment around human being.	: Socio-economic transformation on area basis-covering all people in a given area or concentrating only on a particular group of people normally neglected and in need of help.
(vii) Development of Human Beings	: Conscious raising, awakening, organising, recording of priorities to suit social justice, redeeming the past and opening doors to opportunities to the oppressed and the exploited.

Approaches 1 to 6 are related to delivery system and 7 is basically related the 'receiving mechanism'. However, the voluntary agencies generally follow four clear cut strategies. These are :

Strategy - I	: Simple charity, supplementing welfarism of the state.
Strategy - II	: Encouraging people's participation and in implementing programmes launched by the Government for larger benefit of the community or village.
Strategy - III	: Involving people in programme planning, raising resources, implementing activities and sharing fruits of development.
Strategy - IV	: Conscience instilling and organising people enabling them to demand and undertake planning and implementation of development programmes beneficial to them.

It is evident that voluntary agencies adopting strategy-I generally suffer from inferiority complex and a feeling of helplessness. It is based on 'giver and receiver' relationship. Most people believe that it is paternalistic in nature and cause human degradation—not upliftment of human spirit. The active role of voluntary agencies is limited to the last two strategies. Most voluntary agencies are following these two strategies with varying degree of success. The choice of strategy depends on the ideology, motivation, capability of the organisation, experience of the workers and the actual situation in a given area.[14]

The voluntary organisations have got very wide scope of functions in uplifting women's status. But unfortunately they have not realised the potentialities that they have as pressure groups. The public also has become so dependent on the government for the solution of even those problems which can be tackled by the people themselves. However, the voluntary organisation have to make sincere efforts to re-establish themselves as powerful agencies to fight the deep rooted social evils for which they need committed and dedicated worker. Unless the voluntary organisations take an active part in the movement of liberation of women, merely governmental agencies cannot achieve the desired results.

Concluding Remarks

The voluntary agencies have to bring about a healthy environment for the steady progress. The provision of inputs in the right time and in required quantities may be important, but no less important is the change in the attitude of the people towards development. There is need for external animators to create awareness of a better life outside the rural scene and to sustain interest and participation in the face of social tension that are bound to emerge whenever programmes for the welfare are intensified.

The role of voluntary agencies needs to be emphasized. The role is not of middleman but of midwife. All the voluntary agencies may not be able to provide assets or direct services to the target group they are serving. But, the voluntary agencies may help the people take advantage of the opportunities available to them. There is need for promoting development consciousness among the people. The voluntary agencies alone can undertake this important but time consuming task.

One important reason because of which the voluntary agencies have entered the development field is that rural development administration is far from satisfactory. The delivery system is imperfect. Most developing countries have not yet evolved an appropriate institutional set-up to help the rural poor. The need of the hour is to adopt administration to rural needs. We shall, therefore, study, in the next chapter, the imperfections, associated with rural development administration.

REFERENCES

1. In this context, the report of the team for the Study of Community Projects and National Extension Service, Committee on Plan Projects (Coop.) Vol. Nos. I, II, III, Planning Commission, New Delhi, 1957. *Report of the Study team on Social Welfare and Welfare of Backward Classes*, Government India, 1959, *Block Level Plans and Programmes for Rural Development by Participation of Voluntary Organisations*, *Voluntary Action*, XX-1, 1978 and the successive five year plan documents may be of interest.
2. *Draft Five-Year Plan* (1978-83), Govt. of India, 1978, and the Drart of the *Sixth Five-Year Plan* (1980-85), Govt. of India, 1980.
3. A discussion on the concepts of voluntary organisation and voluntary action is provided in D.P. Chowdhry's *Voluntary* Sacial Welfare in India, Sterling Pub. (S) Ltd., New Delhi, 1971 ; B.K. Roy Burman, *Role of Voluntary Organisation in the Welfare of the Tribals* (Mimeo), Min. of Home Affairs, Govt. of India, 1968, V.M. Kulkarni, Voluntary Action in a Developing Society, IIPA. New Delhi, 1969.
4. D. Paul Chowdhry (1985) ; *Profile of Social Welfare and Development in India*, M.N. Pub. & Distributors, New Delhi. p. 225,
5. Ibid ; p. 226
6. Ibid ; p. 226
7. Ibid ; p. 226
8. Archana Sinha, (1978), *The Social and Political Philosophy of Sarvodaya*, Janaki Prakashan Patna-4, p. 194.

9. Jayaprakash Narayan (1978), *Towards Total Revolution*, Vol. I, p. 144.

10. B.G. Verghese (1979) ; 'Voluntary Action : A New Mission for the New Missionaries', in R.P. Mishra & K.V. Sundaram (Ed. 1979), *Rural Area Development : Perspectives and Approaches*, Sterling Publishers Pvt. Ltd., New Delhi, p. 235.

11. M.S.A. Rao (Ed. 1978), *Social Movements in India*, Vol. I, ' Peasant & Backward Classes Movements', Manohar Publications, New Delhi-2, p. x.

12. R.P. Mishra (Ed. 1978), *op, cit.*, p. 62.

13. Yojana, November 1984, p. 46.

14. *Ibid*, p. 47.

12. WOMEN POWER--WHERE IT GOES FROM HERE ?

Ashok Kumar

Introduction

FOR centuries, women have remained caloistered and confined within the four walls of the home, and dismissed as "the second sex". Here is one very gloomy script for the future. Suppose in the next few years things do not go well, the arms race speeds up, inflation is not contained, and oil supplies are periodically threatened. In order to increase defence spending, hard fought for benefits are nibbled away-first welfare and nutrition programmes, then legal aid, Medical aid, unemployment benefits, disability insurance, housing programmes, vocational education, schools and the arts. These are all drastically cut, and gradually the government hands over the responsibility for social planning to local governments..

However, a clear vision of an alternative future may speed that turn around and provide sustenance when the going gets tough. Here are some ideas in that view to help make tomorrow as a part of the search for women's positive future.

First, barriers between generations will be reduced where all ages go to school, participate in productive life and enjoy periodic leisure. Models for the future in the market are already being tested here or abroad.

To make this change of employment pattern workable, schools must be restructured to provide life long education. Since classes would necessarily be inter generational-knowledge and skills could more easily be transferred from one generation to the next, reducing the load on the teachers. But none of this will be possible unless there is a functioning full employment policy. There will be no end to rationales for limiting competition for scarce jobs from the old, young, minorities and women.

In the foregoing chapters an attempt has been made to study the educational and employment structure of women in India in the present system. In proportion to the female population of India they will remain the elite-head and shoulders above the masses, who either do not have any schooling at all or drop out at various levels of instruction for lack of opportunities as in rural areas, through poverty and social customs.[1] That this growing womenpower is not mobilised and used for national development and well being by our planners is a known fact. Under the circumstances we cannot rest content with saying that we did not create this world or, as the song goes, the future's not ours to see. On the other hand, the present has a responsibility, which is to plan for tomorrow.[2] However, an individual, as well as a nation, plans for the future to reach certain defined goals.

The 20th Century in India or at least the first half of it, is characterised by woman's struggle to assert herself as a human being and to gain recognition in society. Indian society in the last century, and perhaps down the ages, had little regard or use for its girls and women.

Since the beginning of the colonial period, the Indian

education was job-oriented i.e. towards producing clerical staff for the East India Company's successor government. The system is our educational heritage and we hug it with reverence in spite of the changes contemplated in our constitution and plans and the recommendations made by successive commissions for reforms. The reason for introducing the English medium was to meet the need for a clerical staff both in the administration and professions. With the attainment of independence, the need for a different orientation became imperative, but hardly any effort has been made to change the structure and pattern of education or relate it to the manpower needs of the developing economy. There have been additions to the old structure but hardly enough to meet our changing needs.

The multiplicity of institutions of higher education, their uneven distribution, with concentration in urban areas and the utter lack of them in rural areas are well-known facts. In consequence, expansion has added to the unemployment and created social distress and individual frustration, leading to violence and anti-social activities. The reports of employment exchanges prove the waste or misuse of scarce resources to satisfy regional vanity and political ambitions. For instance, conditions in Kerala, which has a high literacy rate and a relatingly highly educated population. In no other State are the consequences of uncoordinated education. When we discuss the plan for tomorrow, the present state of purposelessness and educated unemployment cannot be ignored. While this effects men and women equally, it has a special significance in the advancement of women and the use of womenpower for national and community welfare and development.

Planning for Tomorrow

The need for planning becomes imperative when resources are scarce and strict economy has to be exercised to obtain the desired results.[3] It also becomes imperative when a system, be it education, industry or agriculture, becomes so maladjusted to current requirements that it has to be changed or modified to meet changed circumstances. As far as higher education for girls in India is concerned, resources are limited, priorities sadly lack urgency and the system is outdated and practically irrelevant to the revolutionary change we are anxious to usher in. Hence, to mobilise existing resources and cut out the dead wood of outdated organisation, we need to plan.[4]

We have to bear in mind certain important factors in planning for tomorrow. The first is that we provide more and more education for girls and women. One of the things that is causing grave concern to planners is the wide gap indicated in Chapter 2 of this book between the education of boys and girls. It is observed that the proportion of girls to boys at the primary level is 2 : 5, at the secondary level 1 : 3 and at the university level it is 1 : 4. Even this fails to take note of the fact that there are drop-outs, and high drop-outs among girls than boys, more in rural than in urban areas. Just providing schools is not enough. Nor is it enough to have impressive enrolment figures. The average of drop-outs varies from school to school, district to district and State to State. The reasons are many ; we are concerned about it because of its impact on higher education. To a large extent causes are economic. Perhaps the problem can be met by having better education and a greater earning capacity for women by the acquisition of new techniques and skills.[5] Economic backwardness, when it reaches desperate dimensions, deprives of victim of motivation. The vicious circle begins.[6]

Thus, even when we are concerned with the problem of women's education and its future, we have to note the dismal background of the problem itself. The relevance of education as an investment has yet to be appreciated by the category which needs it most, namely, women.[7]

An Over-view

Different models, including the ILO and other individual scholars, would yie d different projections. But each could be used to make some qualitative points. The ILO population projections for a given country are usually prepared on the basis of assumptions on expected trends in fertility and mortality. While it may be expected that detailed knowledge of the interaction between these factors and the various social and economic characteristics of a country would do better population projections, the evolution in the fertility and mortality trends is in most cases sufficiently gradual for the use of basic assumptions as to future trends to have enabled the statistician to make population projections which have proved useful to many in the analysis of the world's population and its expected evolution.[8]

Similarly, to establish sound projections of the labour force for any country (given the population projections), one would equally wish to take full account of the relationships between labour force participation rates and number of factors determining the evolution of these rates, such as expected changes in school enrolment, retirement age, urban/rural migration, etc., on one hand, and plans for economic and social development and expected rates of economic growth on the other.[9] But firstly, most of the necessary information is generally lacking and very few countries, if any, have actually prepared labour force projections. Projections undertaken in the 1960s were unfortunately made, for lack of knowledge of actual relationship, on the assumption of constant labour force participation rates. Secondly, labour force participation rates, like many other social characteristics, vary only gradually and, therefore, assumptions on their future variation based on past experience are not likely to lead to wide errors in the projections.

Until more information is available, for example, as regards the influence on the levels of labour force participation rates of various economic and social factors—such as the effect of implementation of economic and social development plans, changes in the education system, changes in labour legislation, and so forth a method of projection of the labour force which is to be capable of application to all countries of the world is bound to be based on a solid statistical analysis of past tendencies. The method used in the projection by the ILO has been developed on such a basis.

However, for the projection of 1975-2000, the ILO has done some major modification. A major modification introduced is the use of regression equations as the main projection vehicles, rather than the models used in the above mentioned projection series. In brief, the methods employed are in large measure based on the results of comparative analysis in which statistical, graphical and computer techniques are extensively used. The most important new feature of the latest methodology is the derivation of regression equations which take account also of the trends in rates of change of labour force participation ratios. It is possible that, in a particular country, the future trends in activity rates may diverge to some extent from the path which, for purpose of the present projections, they have been deemed most likely to follow. For instance, they may diverge as a result of more rapid industrialisation and urbanisation or faster increase in school attendance, or introduction of an earlier retirement age than implicity assumed, or as a result of other special factors.[10] The present projection methodology of the ILO was systematically tested by reverse projection techniques. But, for certain countries which had undergone important changes in political, social and economic structure, for these countries, it was necessary to modify somewhat the standard projection methodology.

Standard labour force projections are made by extrapolating time-series observations of age-sex specific participation rates, without consideration of the determinants of these trends. These have often seriously under-estimated the growth in the participation rate of women in recent years, producing errors in the assumptions used in the setting of macro-economic and labour market policies, in measuring the success or failure of women in the labour market, and in predicting the costs of employment-conditioned programmes.[11] However, in the present section attention will be focused on some of the models so far used for forecasting female labour force.

The Bureau of Labour Statistics (BLS) have developed a somewhat different type of model. A projection model that integrates information from various studies of the determinants of labour force participation is provided and applied to the projection of the growth in the labour force of prime-age (25-54) women through 1990. Finally, some lessons are presented from this analysis for assessing the latest BLS projection and for directing future labour supply research towards the improvement of labour force projections.

A paper by Wachter (1977)[12] makes a strong case for including a measure of the desired or anticipated standard of living of an age cohort, along with its actual income. He argues that participation is stimulated when family income is low relative to the expectations formed on the basic of individuals own past experience and observations of the standard of living achieved by others In addition, the potential wages of members of an age cohort are negatively related to the size of the cohort. Hence, members of the postwar baby boom face lower standards of living than they had anticipated, which, in turn, influenced more women in that cohort to participate in the labour force (and bear fewer children). He predicts that the participation rate of each female group between aged 20-64 will continue to rise. His projections through 1986 for ages 35-44 and 45-54 are each about 4 points higher than the BLS projections. One apparent shortcoming is that he still relies on a trend term, although that term's importance is considerably less than in the traditional time-series equation. Another problem is that he does not distinguish between the wage rates of men and women.

The most recent estimates of the participation-unemployment relation are in Perry (1977).[13] Perry also estimates a time-series model that includes aggregate real wages and finds that it does not have a positive, significant effect on most groups' participation rates. However, Perry includes two trend terms in the same equation. Wachter (1977),[14] in his comments, discussed this and other problems with Perry's specification.

An estimate of Cain-Dooley and Ashenfelter-Heckman (1972)[15] covered only prime-age married women. He has assured that the percentage of prime-age women who are married does not change between 1975 and 1990. The projections can be interpreted as conditional forecasts of the growth in the labour force of the proportion change. Assuming that other factors do not interact with the influence of own-wages and husband's income.

Linda Waite (1977),[16] a sociologist at the University of Illinois, Urbana-Campaign, has analysed the impact of changes in sex-role attitudes on female labour force growth. Her preliminary estimates suggest that, even if no further changes occur in individual attitudes, simply the replacement of the older cohorts, who have more conservative views, would add 2 to 4 points to the participation rate by 1990.

To make a 15 years or 20 years participation rate projection, it is not clear from the above mentioned studies that how far back one should go to estimate their trend but it is clear that this decision is critical. Most of the time-series analyses of the discouraged worker effect, which typically use a cyclical term and a trend variable are subject to some criticism if used for long term projections. A solution to the trend extrapolation problem would be to develop a projection model which incorporated the behavioural relationships that underline the year to year changes in each group's participation. Short of the complete estimation of such a model, the results of analyses of various determinants of participation could be used at least to supplement extrapolations in two ways. First, they could be useful in selecting from among alternative projections. Second, they could guide the user of trend of extrapolations in making alternative projections that took into account new information about the paths of variables that influence participation.

In a projection model, Smith (1979)[17] has considered both the aspects i.e. demographic as well as behavioural. He has taken the changes in the total size and age distribution of the population as an exogenous and collected from Census Bureau Projections. For simplicity, he has begun by assuming that, within each age group, the distribution by marital status and presence of children is constant. In fact, however, exogenous increase in the proportion of the female population within each age group that never married or that is childless, for example, would probably increase the size of the female labour force, since never-married and childless women have higher participation rates than women in the same age group who are married or who have young children. The determinants of changes in the group-specific participation rates, particularly the rate among married women, have been the subject of many analyses by economists and sociologists and their results are reflected in Smith's model.

However, the projection model of Smith takes these factors into account. He has defined *L* as the change in the female labour between the base year (*0*), and the projection year (t), *L* as the labour force size of group *i* in a year *t*, *P*.s as its population size, and (*L*/*P*) as its participation rates. Then, where the groups are delineated by age, marital status, and family status and are mutually exclusive.[18] Each group's projected labour force growth or decline is associated with changes in its participation rate and in its population size.

$$\Delta(L/P)i = b1i \, \Delta \, Wi + b2i \, \Delta \, Hi + b3i \, \Delta \, Ni + b4i \, \Delta \, Ei + b5i \, \Delta Ai + b7i \, \Delta \, u + b8i \, \Delta T$$

The first three variables on the right-hand side of the above equation are measures of the expected growth in potential sources of incomes to women in that group : own real wages (W_l). wages of husband or other members of the income-sharing unit (H_i), and non-earned income (N_i). These are the variables that standard neoclassical theory suggest. The coefficient on W_i can be positive or negative depending on whether the substitute or income effect dominates ; most studies of women's participation behaviour have found that the positive substitution effect dominates. The coefficient on other sources of income, b_{2i} and b_{3i} should be negative.

The next two variables measure changes in the group's average educational attainment (*E*) and work-related attitudes (*A*) ; the coefficients on each should be positive. The next variable, *u* is a cyclical variable which may reflect variations in job market conditions either for the group or for the entire labour force. If it is measured by unemployment, the sign on its coefficient should be negative.

The final variable, a time trend (*T*), is included to depict the net effect of omitted variables which themselves, are expected to increase or decrease systematically over time. The major purpose of the trend term in this model was to provide an alternate means of projecting the participation rates of groups for which there is insufficient behavioural information on which to base a projection. In this event, the trend extrapolation method is the recourse.

However, equations should be viewed as covenient framework for integrating the available information on the determinants of participation rate change. It is not set forth as a rigorous forecasting model but rather a first stage in identifying the elements. This model has presented estimates of the effects of wage and unemployment changes only. Thus, this projection model is partial one.

In India, over a period of time a number of studies on estimating stock of different categories of manpower have been conducted by the Planning Commission, different organisations at national and State levels, by the various *ad hoc* committees, individual scholars and working groups set up from time to time. However, it may be noticed that most of these studies pertain to scientific and technical personnel and a very few deal with women work force, general education and educated women.

In an article 'Projecting India's Population to A.D. 2001', Goon and Chandra (1982)[19] has projected the India's population upto 2001. The technique they have used for the projection of the Indian population is the so-called component method based on Kepfitz (1977) models in which they have taken all the three components of population growth, *viz.* fertility, mortality and migration into account. In this book the population is projected by a number of stages after obtaining life tables from RGO office which is given in the Table 12.1, 12.2, and 12.3 below.

So far as these figures are concerned, their projections seem to have been fairly good, if we note that the projected population for 1981 relates to a date (April 1) separated by a calendar month from the reference date (March 1) of the 1981 Census. In this book, they have calculated the male-female ratio for the 1981 census population which is almost same as indicated in the 1981 census. This lends weight to their whole set of projections.

TABLE 12.1

Projected Population of India, by Age & Sex, 1991

Age Group	Population (in thousands)		
	Male	Female	Total
0—4	52612	49634	102246
5—9	50517	48285	98802
10—14	48788	47045	95833
15—19	46684	45308	91997
20—24	38139	32675	70814
25—29	36744	31394	68168
30—34	30606	29640	60246
35—39	25977	26808	52785
40—44	22356	23343	45699
45—49	19275	19511	38786
50—54	16362	15750	32112
55—59	13505	12328	25833
60—64	10625	9345	19972
65—69	7623	6334	15957
70—74	4986	3781	8747
75—79	2967	2064	5031
80—84	1653	1070	2723
85—89	759	508	1267
90—94	192	140	332
95+	12	10	22
Total	430394	404973	835367

Source : Manpower Journal, Vol. XVIII, No. 2 July-September, 1982, pp. 40-42.

TABLE 12.2

Projected Population of India, by Age & Sex, 1996

Age group	Population (in thousands)		
	Male	Female	Total
0–4	55334	52202	107536
5–9	50874	48634	99508
10–14	49542	47844	97386
15–19	47966	46752	94718
20–24	45921	44982	90903
25–29	37504	32343	69847
30–34	36148	30970	67118
35–39	30070	29097	59167
40–44	25495	26049	51544
45–49	21844	22390	37072
50–54	18589	18483	44234
55–59	15529	14744	30273
60–64	12485	11294	23779
65–69	9197	7730	16927
70–74	6118	4676	10794
75–79	3733	2588	6321
80–84	2089	1332	3421
85–89	973	585	1558
90–94	259	163	422
95+	22	15	37
Total	469692	442873	912565

Source : Same as for Table 12.1.

TABLE 12.3

Projected Population of India, Age & Sex, 2001

Age group	Population (in thousands)		
	Male	Female	Total
0—4	58870	55538	114408
5—9	53774	51376	105150
10—14	50173	48291	98464
15—19	49028	47608	96636
20—24	47470	46501	93971
25—29	45424	44642	90066
30—34	37080	32004	69084
35—39	35715	30507	66228
40—44	29684	28404	58082
45—49	25083	25141	50224
50—54	21268	21378	42646
55—59	17856	17488	35344
60—64	14562	13672	28234
65—69	11000	9429	20429
70—74	7535	5743	13278
75—79	4716	3228	7944
80—84	2703	1687	4390
85—89	1264	736	2000
90—94	340	189	529
95+	31	18	49
Total	513576	483580	997156

Source : Same as for Table 12. 1

Projection of Educated Women

In the present study projections for 1990 and A.D. 2000 have been made by making certain sets of assumptions in respect of enrolment targets, wastage and stagnation rates, attrition rates, etc. These have been worked out by broad levels of education. Our object here is not to present the precise figures of the likely stock of educated manpower by sex but to indicate the broad dimension so as to facilitate decisions regarding the expansion of educational facilities after examining the adequacy of the stock in the light of the growing socio-economic demand for education and to consider its cost factors.

The stock estimates are presented at quinquennial intervals. The time horizon of fifteen years henceforth has been selected with a most pragmatic approach keeping in view the long lead time involved in formulation and implementation of any alternate educational strategy. The outturn figures are worked out by applying appropriate wastage/stagnation rates to the estimated enrolment figures of different levels of education.

Since the entire educational system. in our country, presents by and large a pyramidical structure, the enrolment at each subsequent stage is dependent upon the enrolment at its preceding stage except for the intake in various professional courses where there are some other considerations (the economic demand and the government's developmental plans and programmes etc.) which regulate the enrolment policy for the professional courses. Hence, so far as the general education is concerned, the trend based projections of enrolment on the basis of appropriate transition rates have been made whereas for professional courses, the intake targets are independently fixed keeping in view the labour market conditions.

The steps involved in the exercise of projecting the educated women up to A.D. 2001 are :

(i) determining enrolment/intake targets for the different levels/course of education up to the year 2001 and working out the likely outturn for the different years in each education level giving the due allowance for wastage and stagnation on the basis of past trends. This involves :

— fixing enrolment targets and ratios at primary level of education and then determining the flow from primary education level to the subsequent stages by developing appropriate transition ratios ;
— projecting enrolment of different classes of school/college level of education ;
— studying the faculty-wise distribution of enrolment at college stage ;
— estimating the outturn of each stage of education upto the year of 2001.

(ii) extending the series of stock estimates for the years 1971-81 upto the year 2001 by adding the projected out turn figures and duly allowing for attrition of stock on account of mortality and emigration.

The projection thus, worked out and are presented in Table 12.4 & 12.5. The statistical and methodological issues faced in building up the stock series upto A.D. 2001 for each category by sex are discussed in the following subsequent sections.

The data regarding literates by sex for the year 1971 and 1981 have been determined on the basis of information available from census, checking their consistency with the figures of earlier censuses. The relationship between the number of all literates for the years 1971 and 1981 and the estimated stock by sex with qualification upto primary level and above was studied in terms of the percentages. As the same was noted to have steadily increased during these two points, the percentages for the intervening period were interpolated by establishing the straight line relationship.

The distribution of population by educational level and sex up to A.D. 2001 and estimated stock of graduates and above in general and professional education by sex up to A.D. 2001 are presented in Tables 12.4 and 12.5 respectively. Table 12.4 reveals that a total of 48.5 million educated people will be available by A.D. 2001 out of which 18.1 million or a little over one-third (i.e. 37.38 per cent) will be educated women. As far as

TABLE 12.4

Distribution of Population by Educational Level and Sex up to 2001

(In 000's)

Year (Beg.)	Illiterate	Literates						Total
		Below Primary	Primary but below Middle	Middle but below Secondary	Secondary but below Graduates	Graduates and above	Total	
1	2	3	4	5	6	7	8	9
Persons								
1981	436,911	67,653	86,838	56,662	29,093	8,228	248,274	685,185
1986	458,383	73,537	104,248	69,830	41,020	11,020	299,775	758,158
1991	479,925	77,668	122,456	86,022	55,375	15,004	356,525	836,450
1996	496,985	79,668	141,627	105,309	72,312	19,591	418 507	915,492
2001	505,683	78,982	261,555	128,250	92,075	24,934	485,796	991,479
Males								
1981	188,225	42,620	56,535	39,044	21,971	6,003	166,173	354,398
1986	195,045	45,054	65,374	47,632	30,077	8,178	196,315	391,360
1991	201,789	46,420	74,577	58,028	39,513	10,811	229,349	431,138
1996	206,067	45,560	84,095	70,276	50.516	13,859	265,307	471,374
2001	205,845	45,111	93,730	84,748	63,225	17,375	304,189	510,034

Table 12.4 (*Contd.*)

1	2	3	4	5	6	7	8	9
Females								
1981	248,686	25,033	30,303	17,618	7,122	2,025	82,101	330,787
1986	263,338	28,483	38,874	22,198	10,943	2,962	103,460	366,798
1991	278,136	31,248	47,994	27,994	15,862	4,193	127,176	405,312
1996	290,918	33.107	57,532	35,033	21,796	5,732	153,200	444,118
2001	299,838	33,871	67,825	43,502	28,850	7,559	181,607	481,445

TABLE 12.5

Estim ated Stock of Graduates and above in General and Professional Education by Sex up to 2001

(In 000's)

Year	General			Professional			Total		
(Beg.)	Persons	Male	Female	Persons	Male	Female	Persons	Male	Female
1	2	3	4	5	6	7	8	9	10
1981	7,286	5,338	1,948	742	665	77	8,028	6,003	2,025
1986	10,168	7,309	2,859	972	869	103	11,140	8,178	2,962
1991	13,747	9,689	4,058	1,257	1,122	135	15,004	10,811	4,193
1996	18,030	12,468	5,562	1,561	1,391	170	19,591	13,859	5,732
2001	23,032	15,681	7,351	1,902	1,694	208	24,934	17,375	7,559

the availability of women in general and professional education is concerned, a total of 73.51 lakhs and 2.08 lakhs women will be available by completing thier education in general and professional education respectively.

The stock of primary level and above educated persons has been estimated on the basis of the estimated (standardised) enrolment figure of class V for the period 1981-2001 ; and the estimate of all literates based thereupon was derived by applying the percentages obtained by extending the linear relationship. The literacy rates, thus, derived were then cross-checked with estimated literacy rates obtained by fitting the straight line relationship between the literacy rates available at four points of time, i.e. 1951, 1961, 1971 and 1981 as available from different censuses.[20] The comparative results of both the exercises are given below :

TABLE 12.6

Literacy Rates, 1986-2001

Estimated Literacy Rate Based on

Year	Past trends data of four points of time		Relationship between all Literates and the Stock of Primary Level and above	
	Males	Females	Males	Females
1986	50.62	27.40	50.16	28.21
1991	54.17	30.23	53.20	31.38
1996	57.71	33.06	56.28	34.50
2001	61.25	35.89	59.64	37.72

The above two sets of literacy rates are quite close except for the fact that female literacy rates derived on the basis of the relationship between stock of primary level and educated persons and all literates are higher while the literacy rates for males are higher based on the relationship between literacy rate of four points of time. The reason for the higher female literacy rates is the targetted enrolment ratios for future years while for male higher literacy rates, it is because of the trends in past performance being reflected in the linear relationship.

Projection of Women Labour Force

For the present exercise women labour force figures and 1985 unemployment figures are taken from Seventh Five Year Plan 1985-90, Vols. I and II, Planning Commission which is based on NSS 32nd round (usual status) figures. The figures for 1980, 1990 and A.D. 2000 have been computed by applying the unemployment rate for 1985 to the labour force figures of the corresponding year. The data showing labour force based on NSS 32nd round (usual status) and unemployment for the year 1980 and 1985 and the projections for 1990 and A.D. 2000 by age-groups, sex and rural urban location are presented in the Table 12.7.

As per Seventh Five Year Plan the backlog of unemployment at the onset of the plan has been estimated of 9.2 million for the age group of 5 plus. During the plan there would be a further addition of 39.38 million of labour force and there would be additional employment to the tune of 40.36 million. Thus, the unemployed force in 1990 would be 8.22 million persons. During the decade A.D. 1990-2000 it is estimated that there would be an addition of 83.20 million to the labour force. That is, during the decade efforts will have to be made to generate jobs for 91.44 million. Of this, women in age group of 5 plus would constitute 25.29 million and that in 15-59 years age group would be 22.38 million. Of this, 17.58 million would be rural and 4.80 million in urban.[21]

Further, Table 12.7 reveals that a total of 97.23 million in 1990 and 118.36 million by A.D. 2000 women labour force will be available for jobs. Out of which a major portion of women work force, i.e., 80.69 million and 93.45 million in 1990 and 2000 respectively would be in rural areas. Among the different age groups, the major distribution of women work force is in the age of 15-59 years. However, more than 80 per cent of the total women work force is required only in the rural areas by 1990 in all the age groups, whereas it will be less by 2000 in age group of 59 and above. A little over one-fifth, i.e., 22.52 per cent of the total projected work force of 2000 will be from rural areas in the age groups of 59 years and above.

Conclusion

Different projection models, in India and abroad have been developed from time to time for projecting population, labour force and educated manpower. But all the projections more or less are made by extrapolating time-series observations, component approach and by observing linear trends. However, to make a projection of 15 years or 20 years, it is not clear from any of the studies that how far back one should go to estimate their trend. Most of the time-series analyses of the discouraged worker effect, which typically use a cyclical term and a trend variable are subject to the criticism if used for long-term projections. A solution to trend extrapolation problem would be to develop a projection model which incorporated the behavioural relationship that underlie the year to year changes in each group's participation. Short of the complete estimation of such a model, the results of analyses of various determinants of participation could be used at least to supplement extrapolations in two ways. First, they could be useful in selecting from among alternative projections. Second, they could guide the user of trend extrapolations in making alternative projections that took into account new information about the paths of variables that influence participation.

The data regarding literates by sex for the year 1971 and 1981 have been determined on the basis of information available from census checking their consistency. The relationship between the number of all literates for the year 1971 and 1981 and the estimated stock by sex with qualification primary level and above was studied in terms of the percentages. As the same was noted to have steadily increased during these two points, the percentages for the intervening period were interpolated by establishing the straight line relationship. The distribution of population by educational level and sex up to A.D. 2001 is thus estimated and presented in Tables 12.4 and 12.5 The results exhibit that a total of 48.5 million educated persons will be available by A.D. 2001 out of which 18.1 million or a little over one-third (i.e. 37.38 per cent) will be educated women. As far as the availability of women in general and professional education is concerned, a total of 73.51

TABLE 12.7

Table showing Labour force based on NSS 32nd Round (usual status) and Unemployment for the year 1980 and 1985 and the Projections for 1990 and A.D. 2000 by Age Groups and Rural/Urban Location

Year		Age Group In Million			5—15 Years		
		Labour Force	Unemploy-ment	% of Unemploy ment	Labour	Unemploy-ment	% of Unemp-loyment
1	2	3	4	8	6	7	8
1980	Rural Male	148.86	3.24	2.18	9.12	0.17	1.86
	Rural Female	66.24	3.51	5.30	5.88	0.26	4.42
	Urban Male	44.84	3.16	7.05	1.12	0.09	8.04
	Urban Female	10.81	2.11	19.52	0.69	0.08	11.59
1985	Rural Male	164.18	3.74	2.88	9.37	0.18	1.92
	Rural Female	73.21	4.06	5.55	6.14	0.29	4.72
	Urban Male	54.69	3.65	6.67	1.27	0.09	7.09
	Urban Female	13.32	2.44	18.32	0.80	0.08	10.00
1990	Rural Male	180.64	4.32	2.39	9.56	0.19	1.99
	Rural Female	80.69	4.69	5.81	6.27	0.32	5.10

1	2	3	4	5	6	7	8
	Urban Male	66.91	4.22	6.31	1.43	0.09	6.29
	Urban Female	16.54	2.82	17.05	0.91	0.08	8.79
2000	Rural Male	208.52	5.77	2.77	9.58	0.21	2.19
	Rural Female	93.45	6.27	6.71	6.23	0.38	6.10
	Urban Male	101.10	5.63	5.57	3.26	0.07	2.15
	Urban Female	24.91	3.77	15.13	1.18	0.09	7.63

		Age group					
		15-59 Years			59 Years and above		
		Labour Force	Unemployment	% of Unemployment	Labour Force	Unemployment	% of
1	2	9	10	11	12	13	14
1980	Rural Male	128.53	3.04	2.37	11.21	0.03	0.27
	Rural Female	57.73	3.20	5.54	2.63	0.05	1.90
	Urban Male	41.71	3.04	7.89	2.01	0.03	1.49
	Urban Female	9.71	2.03	20.91	0.41	—	—
1985	Rural Male	142.61	3.52	2.47	12.20	0.04	0.33
	Rural Femal	64.18	3.71	5.78	2.68	0.06	2.08
	Urban Male	51.00	3.52	6.90	2.42	0.04	1.65
	Urban Female	12.02	2.35	19.55	0.50	0.01	2.00
1990	Rural Male	157.43	4.00	2.54	13.65	0.13	0.95
	Rural Female	71.18	4.27	5.93	3.24	0.15	4.63

1	2	9	10	11	12	13	14
	Urban Male	62.40	4.00	6.40	3.00	0.13	4 33
	Urban Female	14.99	2.67	17.81	0.64	0.07	10.94
2000	Rural Male	181.32	5.17	2.85	17.62	0.39	2.21
	Rural Female	83.01	5.44	6.55	4.21	0.45	10.69
	Urban Male	92.86	5.17	5.57	4.98	0.39	7.83
	Urban Female	22.66	3.45	15.22	1.07	0.23	21.50

Source : (i) Labour Force figures are from Seventh Five Year Plan, 1985-90 (Vol. I), Planning Commission.
(ii) 1985 Unemployment figures are from Seventh Five Year Plan 1985-90 (Vol. II), Planning Commission.

lakhs women will be available by completing their education in general and professional education respectively.

According to VII Five Year Plan, the backlog of unemployed at the onset of the Plan has been estimated at 9.2 million for the age group of 5 years and above. During the plan, there would be a further addition of 39.38 million to the labour force and there would be additional employment to the tune of 40.36 million. The unemployment, therefore, in 1990 would be 8.22 million persons. During the decade A.D. 1990-2000 it is estimated that there would be an addition of 83.20 million to the labour force. That is, during the decade efforts will have to be made to generate jobs for 91.44 million and that in 15-59 years age group would be 22.38 million. Out of which, 17.58 million would be rural and 4.80 million in urban areas. Further, it is observed that a total of 97.23 million in 1990 and 118.36 million by A.D. 2000, women labour force will be available for jobs. Of this, a major portion of women work force i.e. 80.69 million and 93.45 million in 1990 and 2000 respectively would be in rural areas only. Among the different age groups, the major distribution of women work force is in the ages 15-59 years (see Table 12.7).

REFERENCES

1. YWCA (1971) of India—'The Educated Women in Indian Society Today', Tata McGraw Hill Publishing Co. Ltd., Bombay-New Delhi, p. 248.
2. *Ibid.*, p. 249.
3. *Ibid.*, p. 248.
4. Ralph, E. Smith (1979) : 'Projecting the size of the Female Labour Force : what makes a difference ?', in ed, book of Lloyd, Andrews & Gilroy, Women in the Labour Market, Columbia University Press, New York.
5. *Ibid.*, p. 65.
6. *Ibid.*, p. 59.
7. *Ibid.*, p. 52.
8. ILO (1973); Labour Force Projections, Part VI.
9. *Ibid.*, p. 24.
10. ILO (1977) : Labour Force Estimates and Projections, 1950-2000, Geneva, pp xi-xii.

11. Ralf, E. Smith (1979): op. cit., p. 45.
12. Howard, Fullerton and Paul Flain (1976) : 'New Labour Force Projections to 1990', Monthly Labour Review 99, No. 12, pp. 3-13.
13. A.R. Gallant (1975): 'Testing a Subset of Parameters of a Non-linear Regression Model', Journal of the American Statistical Association 70, No. 352, pp. 927-32.
14. Andrew, Sun (1977) : 'Female Labour Force Participation : Why Projections have been Too Low'. Monthly Labour Review 100, No. 7, pp. 18-24.
15. R.S. Pindyck & D. Rubenfield (1976) : Econometric Models and Forecasts, McGraw-Hill, New York.
16. Smith (1979): op. cit., p. 60.
17. *Ibid.*, p. 48.
18. Derivation :
19. A.M. Goon & N.K. Chandra (1982) : 'Projecting India's Population to 2001 A.D.', Manpower Journal, Vol. xviii, No. 2, July-September, pp. 19-42.
20. *Ibid.*, p. 35.
21. K.L. Rawal & J.A. Dadlani (1987) : 'Women and Employment', unpub. Background Seminar paper, Organised by IAMR-ICNUN on Dev. of Wcmen as Human Resource, September 12-13, pp. 24. 25.

Index